PLEIADIAN CODE
III

ALIEN FRAGMENT

EVA MARQUEZ

DEDICATION

To YOU,
in the future.

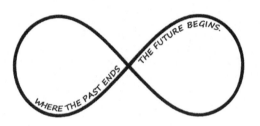

ACKNOWLEDGEMENTS

With great love and joy, I share the final book in the Pleiadian Code trilogy: Pleiadian Code III, Alien Fragment. Beyond what words can express, I am grateful for this opportunity to share with you the channeled messages from the Pleiadians and other benevolent beings of this Universe.

I am grateful to my family for supporting and assisting me on this journey.

My heartfelt thanks to all my friends and clients. Your constant support and inspiration are the driving forces behind every book I write. I am truly grateful for your role in this journey. May you be blessed with happiness, good health, abundance, and always be surrounded by unconditional love.

I give a special heartfelt thank you to my friend and editor-in-chief for this book, Katie Bowerbank. Thank you for all those long hours, Zoom conferences, and brainstorming and for truly listening with your heart to what I was trying to say when I could not find the proper English words to keep the story as authentic as I felt it in my soul. May your own book be successful beyond your wildest expectations.

I also want to give a big heartfelt thank you to Rodrigo Pincheira for his kindness in offering to edit this book. It means a lot to me. It has been a rough year, and I wish you and your family the future you dream about.

My deepest gratitude goes to my friend and True Teacher, Ann. Pleiadian Code I, The Great Soul Rescue, came as a download in your kitchen. Pleiadian Code III, Alien Fragment, marks where the past ends and the future begins. There is so much ahead of us, and I know you have new teachings ready. Thank you for believing in me and for your patience in guiding me to change my life path. May you and your family always be blessed.

Thank you to Michael Nagula, AMRA Publishing, and everyone on their team.

May you all be blessed with positive abundance and unconditional love. Thank you! Thank you! Thank you!

Table of Contents

FOREWORD

Pleiadian Code I, The Great Soul Rescue, has assisted you in healing the human.

Pleiadian Code II, Cosmic Love has assisted you in falling back in love with who you are (falling back in love with the alien you are) and relearning how to thrive on Earth.

Pleiadian Code III, Alien Fragment navigates you to the next step of your spiritual growth and guides you through your evolution from the three-dimensional human being into the fifth-dimensional (or beyond) multi-planetary being that you used to be during your time in Atlantis or Lemuria.

The lessons you learn in this book will manifest into your everyday life. The essence of your soul will awaken the alien memories you have left hidden in the Knowledge Keepers of the Earth. You will notice that while your body is resting at night, your soul will journey to other worlds where you are taught by true teachers. This triggers the human ego within you, and you may again be attacked with negative energy, destructive thoughts, and feelings of giving up. Keep persisting. You have almost reached the golden realm of the fifth-dimensional frequency. When you do, you will access your alien mind and thrive in the third-dimensional human body to enjoy a life of happiness, love, good health, and success while serving humanity.

You are invited to become a part of the story throughout these pages while holding compassion for Maggie and Mikael. If you choose to, you will be assisted by the Council of Light and Dark from Sirius A. This book is thoughtfully woven with stories and wisdom teaching. The alien compass and alien fragment will become new words within your spiritual vocabulary. You will learn how to master the 5D Virus Zone and some of the history of the Galactic Wars. This is the story of your soul's journey to Earth, and you will discover your return ticket to your home in the Universe.

The story of Maggie and Mikael tells the tale of star-seed beings living on Earth who have forgotten who they were. They struggle and feel different, just as you do. Yet, they are brave in the pursuit of their calling. Higher beings elevate them from their meditations and night dreams into their worlds on Sirius, Orion, and Pleiades. They start teaching them so that they can accomplish their mission on Earth, as agreed upon in their pre-birth soul contract. Once again, unconditional love helps to overcome all obstacles. Miraculous healing is accessible to all willing to accept it, you included. Where the past ends, the future beings. May your future be spectacular. Let the TRANSFORMATION begin.

We love you unconditionally ~ Pleiadians, Orions, and Sirians ~ The Lights of the Universe.

CHAPTER 1

WISDOM TEACHING

"You are the Light, and you are the Dark, and it is your mission to harmonize these forces within you so that you can return home to the Universe." - Lights of the Universe.

TURQUOISE GARDEN
Sirius Transmission

"Here is the essence of your soul," said the True Teacher as she looked over her students.

Every night, the students' souls would gather in the temple on Sirius A, where the teacher imparted wisdom teachings, hoping they would remember in their awakened state.

"In the turquoise-colored rose?" someone asked.

"The rose is just one precious thing that you remember from your galactic past that is still alive in the future. This rose came from the stars, just as you did," she smiled at them, "The rose will help you remember our connection to each other."

She took out a tiny bottle and sprayed the essence of the rose into the air.

"Approximately 2,000 years ago, our souls met here, on Sirius, in our astral bodies. It was on the last day of Christ's crucifixion. Our soul's unity carried us here. On Earth, we were known as the Essenes. Others on the Earth were connected to us at that time in different geological locations, known by different names. Yet, in our souls, we were all united with the Christ/Magdalene consciousness, with the Essenes."

"During our meeting on Sirius, we learned that our task on Earth was far from complete and that we needed to leave a reminder for our future selves so that we would never forget who we are, what our task is, and most importantly - so that we would remember each other."

"The HEART of humanity was awakened at Christ's crucifixion."

"The MIND of humanity is awakening now," she silently said as she looked at each of them. The future is now."

She paused and energetically transmuted as much unconditional love into their souls as she could so that they would remember later in their waking lives.

"In the Turquoise Garden rests the essence of your soul. You will need it to heal your alien mind so that you can guide humanity into fifth-dimensional awareness."

"We planted the roses in the Turquoise Garden and buried the Christ/Magdalene consciousness with turquoise essence in the Earth. As above, so below.

Close your eyes and open the inner eye of your soul. Travel within your mind to a rose garden in full bloom. Breathe in the sweet scent of the roses. Hear the gentle whispers in the air. Fill your whole being with the turquoise essence and hear its lovely sound. Acknowledge your human ego and show it the staircase to your brilliant mind. As above, so below. As in the Cosmos, so on the Earth. The Turquoise Garden is your safe place where your infinite soul and alien mind unite."

They all sat silently, and she could see their rainbow bodies glowing brilliantly through her inner vision.

"You've always believed in the power of love. Love overcomes any obstacles. When you love, you live. When you love, you heal. Love will lead you to find each other."

LIFE ON EARTH
Lights of the Universe Transmission

Eons ago, you came from the stars. Eventually, you became the human you are today. In Atlantis, lowering your vibration resulted in the separation of consciousness, which led to disconnection from oneness. The Light and Dark sides became more visible in the duality template on Earth, and within a short time, darkness prevailed with a hunger for power. It poisoned the brilliant mind, and the codes of light that are encoded in the souls of every being became hidden. However, light codes were put in a safe place for those who abandoned their spiritual practices to help them retain higher consciousness when ready.

Did the Earth become a gold cage, and did divine beings become exotic birds captured inside?

Yes.

Is Earth a cruel place?

No.

Everything on Earth is here to teach you.

Once you turn the hate of life on Earth into the love of life, you will see that the cage door has always been open. Higher consciousness has always been here, always available to earnest wisdom seekers. Be brave, rise from 3D, explore, learn, and thrive in 5D, and be happy before leaving the Earth. Happiness and unconditional love fit well with your alien mind.

DUALITY TEMPLATE
Sirian Transmission

This Universe is part of the duality of Light and Dark. None of us remember what it was like before that. This Universe, as we know it today, was a harmonious merge between Cosmic Love, the soul group that discovered it, and the Intelligent Mind, the pre-existing energy of this Universe, before combining with the Cosmic Love soul group. What is Light, and what is Dark?

Is Cosmic Love a safe haven for the soul, a source of light? Or is it dark because it entered this Universe that was initially just an Intelligent Mind? Is it dark because it merged with an intelligent mind and manifested duality to satisfy its natural passion and curiosity about life?

Or is the Intelligent Mind a source of light because it has the knowledge and skills to survive in this Universe? Does this Intelligent Mind know that our Universe could equally be a part of other Universes in the whole of existence, considering that hardly any extraterrestrial could explain it in a language that could be understood? Or is it dark because it has rules, laws, and natural order to ensure survival? Could it be dark because it could not resist the original union with the soul and assisted in creating a third particle, the body? In this body, could they have this experience as female and male, as light and dark, as two opposite particles that attract each other?

In our definition, the soul is the light of God (oneness), and the mind is a dark, safe cocoon meant to keep the soul safe on its journey. But on any journey, there may be unexpected troubles, and when the mind gets infected, a safe cocoon can shift into a bed of dangerous thorns to protect its rose.

MOTHER EARTH'S TEACHING
Pleiadian Transmission

The sun gives you light on Earth to live, create, grow food, and thrive. Night surrounds you in darkness so that you can rejuvenate your body. The shroud of darkness protects and surrounds you when you are having a dark night of the soul. Your dark night of the soul can show you how the healing mud at the bottom of the darkness nourishes you into the light. Darkness, in its original essence, is healing. Its healing nature sparks the light of soul remembrance.

As the light of the day and the dark of the night chase each other around the Earth, its function is out of your control, but your emotions are different. You have the ultimate choice of how you choose to feel about anything. So you see, light and dark have always been there, part of you, within you. The knowledge of light and dark is encoded within your DNA. The original Universal duality template is coded in neutral language (energy). It is the foundation of your life, even supporting your life. However, on Earth, you have been conditioned by outside influences that suggest how you should feel and behave, what is expected from you, what is good and what is bad.

On Earth, both light and dark have their champions, and they equally advocate for their agendas with good reasoning. Remember you are living in a place where your senses are heightened, your emotions escalate, and duality presents you with a life of illusions—illusions that create a very real reality for each of you. Your physical body is conditioned by several influences; however, your emotions are the primary keys to your inner program.

On Earth, we all learned that everything can be expressed through the language of emotions. Perhaps the higher force was arranged long ago to encourage extraterrestrial beings to find Earth, conduct experiments, and discover the inner workings and meaning of the duality template. We gained much more than we bargained for. What was thought to be a short stay by our extraterrestrial ancestors turned into eons—not by our wishes but by the forces of destiny. Are you ready to go home?

YOUR SPIRITUAL TEAM
Pleiadian Transmission

We are here to assist in your spiritual and physical transformation from the 3D consciousness into the alien 5D (and higher) consciousness. This means that the human race can rightfully become planetary beings and continue mastering the template in the higher dimensions until they are done. This is a journey for all of us. There are no winners or losers. Some knowledge can be shared, some wisdom must be discovered, and all of the teaching has to be embraced as a new way of living, bonded in unity instead of separation.

Every night, when you sleep, your soul journeys to the higher dimensions, and you often find yourself in our company. You can think of us as your soul family or friends in the cosmos. We can continue to remind you and teach you the purpose of your being in service to humanity. When you transform your life, you inspire others to follow in your footsteps. True teachers teach by example, as Christ and Magdalene did in your not-so-dist past.

CAGE
Maggie's Dream

"I will step out of the cage and open my heart to fully believe that there is more than my human eye can see, more than my ears can hear, and more than my heart can feel right now. Deep inside me, I feel I am more than just a human living an ordinary life. I will heal my mind of the thousand-year-old amnesia to remember who I am, and I will remember that every thought and every action matters. Our thoughts and actions shaped the Earth to where it is today."

In her lucid dream, she heard a voice asking, "How do you feel about this? How do you feel that your thoughts and actions shaped the Earth into what it is today?"

Her courage was suddenly replaced with sweeping fear that she had failed at something. "Uneasy," she slowly answered.

"I will step out of the "cage" of a predestined life and learn how to control my thoughts and actions so that I may better contribute to shaping this world for the tomorrow that is to come, and then return home."

"Don't forget that the connection of the heart and mind is the key. Pay attention to all signs and symbols," the loud voice woke her up.

Maggie sat up wide awake on her bed in the middle of the night. Did someone actually talk to me? I heard this voice before. It felt real. Heart and mind, I can understand that, but what do they mean by signs and symbols?

MAGGIE'S BEINGS - COFFEE SHOP
Maggie's Life

Later that day, while Maggie was making a latte for one of her regular senior customers, she was thinking of her dream. One minute, she felt brave and courageous; another, she was flooded with fears of failure, as if she were responsible for all the Earth's suffering. It reminded her of how she felt in her childhood, how she often felt like a failure. She also believed that she was the reason for everyone else's misery. Maybe the world would be better off if I was not born, she used to think.

Signs and symbols, she thought silently, will I notice them?

"Here is your latte, George."

"You have the magic beans, Maggie. Your coffee always fills me with happiness."

"Thank you," smiled Maggie.

"Love and light to you," said George as he was about to leave. He noticed that Maggie was staring at him blankly, adding, "As the Beatles sang, all you need is love, and as a wise man said, there is always a light at the end of the tunnel. Have a great day, Maggie." He smiled and left.

At that moment, Maggie felt the connection between her mind and her heart, and she started to understand what the voice in her dream was saying to her. She had named her coffee shop Maggie's Beings. Throughout her life, she sensed many invisible beings helping her along her journey; she did not always recognize them, and she used to fear them. Then, when

13

the opportunity came to open her shop, she hoped that these beings would fill the cups of her customers with the love and support they had always shared with her.

For the rest of the day, she wished "love and light" to every customer and didn't care what they thought about her saying it.

CHAPTER 2

KNOWLEDGE KEEPERS

GALACTIC LIBRARIANS
Sirian Transmission

Sirians are known as the galactic librarians, for we are Knowledge Keepers. You also know us as Wisdom Teachers. We have recorded the history of this Universe as far back as extraterrestrials can remember. These records can be accessed within our Akashic Records on Sirius B.

The Earth is a conscious being. It is a living library unique to the other planets in your solar system. It also has the capacity to record its own stories. We discovered how to read from her living energy during our time in Lemuria. Earth is your mother, healer, first teacher, and Knowledge Keeper in your earthly incarnations.

Within your body is another Knowledge Keeper, your DNA. In every incarnation, the soul and ego memories are downloaded into your body alongside your soul contract for that particular life. Therefore, your life is predestined. All of your past memories can be read through the body's energy system, and through this, you can begin to access memories to further your transformation, change your soul contract, and choose a better future for yourself (then it was predestined, yes, you can do that).

Changing your soul contract while already incarnated in the body is a loving gift from Mother Earth. You have always had the choice of how you will lead your life. You believe you are trapped in the cage, yet you cannot see that the cage is not locked. Transforming your old beliefs gives you the courage to open the door and leave that cage.

A Knowledge Keeper is something or someone that stores information within.

In the ancient past, we also created other types of knowledge-keepers. We strategically disbursed some of our extraterrestrial knowledge within Earth's Mineral and Plant Kingdoms for safekeeping in case we need it in the future. Since you are still looking for this information, we wanted to share with you the important parts of your planet's history, such as how the knowledge was kept, how it was accessed, and how you can find it today. Remember, thousands of years have gone by, and a lot has changed, but true knowledge is like unconditional love; it is everlasting.

AKASHIC RECORDS

Books have been written for thousands of years on Earth. Their original purpose was to be the Knowledge Keepers, especially for those who survived the great cataclysm of Atlantis. A book of true knowledge is an heirloom written with the intent that it will serve humanity in future times.

During the Lemurian and Atlantean eraseras, physical books were not needed on Earth. Everything was already recorded in the Akashic Records. Physical books were ancient artifacts, and some ETs did not even remember them.

The Atlantean beings were known for their advanced technology. Every bit of helpful knowledge was stored in "electronic files" that could easily be accessed with what you would call today a wireless network. When your task requires you to have specific information, you would visit this virtual library and download the "information file" into your storage data device, which is similar in function to the Cloud. You would read this file with the assistance of a physical reading device or an internal implant within your body that served this purpose, depending on your preference.

However, it was more challenging than it sounds. The Akashic Records has restrictions, even for extraterrestrial beings. We all have to play by the same rules because knowledge is a power that has been tested countless times. The power given to the wrong mind is a tool for destruction, while it can be a wondrous thing in the right hands. The clearance into the library depends on your level of education, spiritual level, and the sector you are from. The type of clearance you have dictates your access to the Akashic Records and the information contained within. For example, a nuclear engineer does not need access to files on brain surgery, just as a spaceship commander from Rigel does not need access to Wisdom Teaching from Sirius A. Unless the spaceship commander and the nuclear engineer would like to begin a new journey and enroll in a new educational program, at which point there would be proper channels to follow for advancement.

Knowledge is free and universal, and everyone has the opportunity to gain it. Whether you came from the most advanced parts of the Universe or were born here on Earth, a certain level of mastery is required before you are given access to the Akashic Records.

EARTH'S KNOWLEDGE KEEPERS
Pleiadian Transmission

Everything on Earth is automatically recorded in the Mineral Kingdom. In their libraries, you can find answers to all Earthly-related problems and illnesses and all history.

In Lemuria, we discovered that Mother Earth created these energy hot spots where wounded animals would gather to heal. We learned that Earth's healing energy from the crystalline grid supports the living life force. Its healing energy is similar to the healing properties of Mintaka and Pleiades. The crystalline grid lies within the Earth's body and spreads across the surface through ley lines and geometric patterning. This grid is sophisticated and intelligent, and one could call it the mind of Earth. The mind of Earth is similar to the mind of Mintaka.

We have learned that the Earth's crystalline grid is compatible with the energy of the Universal Mind. So we started to think: If we can store and retrieve records in the Akashic Records, which are part of the Universal Mind, there must be a similar way to do the same with the crystalline grid. We understand how unique the Earth is. She is a conscious, living being with a programmable core.

In Atlantis, the Mineral Kingdom had many uses, most notably as:
Record Keepers: Storage devices (utilized by Earth and ET beings).
Amplifiers: Sources of incredible energy – ley lines, vortex, stargate, focused healing energy in Rejuvenating Temples, and directed energetic work, as well as natural power sources (similar to solar power).

Programmable: It could be used for positive and negative effects, and it holds the frequency of the intended program, for example, love, healing, or hate and anger. Minerals do not distinguish or discriminate in energy programs. To them, it is just energy.

Tools: used on their own or in other devices such as electronics, medical devices, cutting tools, etc.

In Lemuria: Vessels for other beings (invisible to your eye).

CRYSTAL KNOWLEDGE KEEPERS
Pleiadian Transmission

In Lemuria, we were one with the Earth and did not need to keep files. In Atlantis, we developed a device we can call a crystal reader to imprint knowledge in crystals on Earth. You had a device that would download files from the Akashic Records and upload them to crystals, creating your own personal library. The same device would retrieve the information from the crystals as needed.

Approximately 6,000 years before Atlantis's destruction, we started noticing disharmony in the Earth's energy, which foretold troubled times ahead. We challenged ourselves to learn how to use crystals without a crystal reading device. How would we use them if our ET technology was without external power?

Life in Atlantis was very comfortable, and we must admit that technology spoiled us, which made life easier. We utilized tools similar to your smartphones, computers, etc. So we took upon ourselves the task of searching back in history to find out how to operate Earth's gifts without using our externally powered technology. We had to rekindle our knowledge of ancient Lemurian abilities to achieve this. We had to re-learn how to be one with the Earth and become one, vibrating with nature again. One can say that Lemurians were true magicians. Their intuitive abilities and ability to merge with the essence of nature and any living being were phenomenal. After a thorough search in history and with significant practice, we mastered the Lemurian abilities and could program crystals using our mind's frequency.

Simply explained, you have a crystal in your pineal gland, in the center of your brain. Let's call this your Master Crystal. When your Master Crystal consciously connects with particular crystals within the Earth, you can transport some of your memory to those crystals. We could preserve sacred knowledge through the magic of divine communion with the Mineral Kingdom. This is where the Lemurian crystal name originates from. If you were part of this task force, the memory of this is sealed within your soul symbol; therefore, only you can retrieve it. Later, wisdom teachers granted access to this sacred knowledge only to certain initiates who earned this privilege. It is important to note that only the Children of the Law of One mastered and used this technique.

SYMBOLS KNOWLEDGE KEEPERS
Sirian Transmission

Since entering our life in Egypt, the painful realization that we may be trapped on Earth for a very long time has settled in. Seers had predicted that our stay here could be for thousands of years. We had to challenge ourselves with a new task: preserving knowledge that will survive into the future. We needed to create a path that would lead us back to ourselves in case we needed to remember our origins or how to read crystal Knowledge Keepers. Master Thoth led us in this endeavor to preserve the knowledge we prepared in Atlantis, intending to withstand the test of time.

There were two main components of this project. First, we wanted to share most of our knowledge so everyone could access it. This would keep us safe from being targeted by other surviving ET groups for hiding the information from them.

Second, we needed to create a new way of communication, a new language that the soul will recognize no matter how many incarnations it will have. We were concerned that our original language might be forgotten for thousands of years. We looked at our current language and considered how we could express our language in symbols since symbols are part of the Language of Light. At that time, at least three different ET languages were spoken around the Earth. For your curiosity, the Sirian language, combined with dark and light energy sounds, was spoken in Egypt and is understood by all ET beings living in Atlantis. The Pleiadians preferred the Language of Light. The Andromedans preferred the language of sound frequencies, and the Orions favored their guttural dialect of the Sirian language.

Since then, we have worked tirelessly to preserve all we know in written form (in words and symbols) in real physical books, which back then were stone tablets. This means that we had to learn how to write. Would you believe we did not know how to physically write?

We created oral storytelling traditions and inspired each other to express sacred teachings through art and music. This way, we could share anything (even our secrets) as they were weaved into riddles that only the initiated would recognize. This new form of knowledge-keeping allowed us to pass our wisdom teachings to future generations. Eventually, the ability to work with Crystal Knowledge Keepers became a secret teaching in Mystery Schools, as the information that survived was not suitable for everyone's use.

Symbols, drawings, art, and music became the primary and most essential sources to remind you of who you are and where you came from because the eyes are the doorway to your soul. When your soul starts remembering, it opens a door for you to all the ancient knowledge you need to remember how to find your way back home. Over those thousands of years, much has changed. Language has changed, but the meaning captured in ancient symbols, drawings, art, and music remains the same.

When you see a picture or symbol or hear sounds that echo ancient truths, you may feel emotions stir inside of you or get teary-eyed. Acknowledge that you are having an emotionally corresponding reaction to what you are seeing, hearing, or sensing at that moment. This emotional reaction is your DNA (your Knowledge Keeper) talking back to you, reminding you of something you once knew.

COMMUNICATION WITH HIGHER DIMENSIONS AND YOUR GUIDES

Sirius Transmission

Symbols became a bridge between the physical and spiritual worlds. They are our favorite way of communicating with you because they are part of the Language of Light, part of the universal truth that cannot be changed. Since you lived when the Language of Light was commonly used, knowledge of the Language of Light is encoded within your DNA. That being the case, you can remember what the symbols mean within your soul. This has been the core of esoteric teachings since ancient Egypt. Symbols are a gentle and safe way to activate the Knowledge Keeper within you. You do not need anyone to whisper words of wisdom in your ears and become codependent on their guidance. By noticing symbols and signs, you can become an investigator in finding their true meaning. In this way, you are working toward gaining your true power (true knowledge) that no one can take away from you.

For example, you may have had visions or dreams about the Ankh, a symbol you may have never seen in this life, yet you feel compelled to create one. Then, randomly, you find a book with a detailed description of this symbol. You get the book, even if it causes financial strain on you because you are thirsty for knowledge about this symbol somewhere inside. We want you to know that there is no such thing as a coincidence. There is an explanation. Your soul recognizes the emblem. You have a past life memory recollection (the symbol activated your ancient DNA), and your soul leads you to more information about it. The Ankh symbol would only have meaning if you remembered it from your past life; otherwise, you would not have even dreamt about it.

The next step is to learn how to intellectually and emotionally understand the symbols' energetic meanings. Emotions can be explained through language (spoken or silent) so that they can be understood by the intellectual mind. (Notice heart-mind connection.) Allow your mind to perceive symbols and signs, but pay attention to your original emotions connected to them. Let your heart (your soul) show you how to find the true meaning of the feeling they awaken within you. Your emotions bring out the memories from your body's Knowledge Keeper. This is how the heart-mind connection works.

Another level of the decoding of symbols comes with decoding the language of colors. This will apply to ancient artwork. Colors are also an original part of the Language of Light. Messages could be expressed through colors. Using colors to draw symbols or create art could tell the right audience a unique story. Look at the symbols and art from ancient Egypt. Pay attention to red, green, and blue (at this time, blue may look very dark blue or black as the paint has aged) and notice their message. You might be surprised how many untold stories you may discover.

In "Pleiadian Code II" we detailed the meaning of red, blue, and green. Here is a little summary:

Red is the color of your ego, your human part, and masculine energy. It represents your thoughts, emotions of the past, and survival.

Green is the color of your soul, your divine part, and feminine energy. It represents your feelings, emotions of the future, and spiritual growth leading into ascension.

Blue is the color of your body, unified energy, and nervous system, which is the Knowledge Keeper of your body (it downloads your DNA information). It represents your will, emotions of the present time, true power, and your godliness.

Embracing this given knowledge, look at the art from ancient Egypt once again (the one that really draws your attention), but this time through the eyes of your soul. Instead of color, see the story of your ego (your thoughts), soul (your feelings), and body (your will). What kind of a message are they relating to you? Perceive it with your mind and use the logical color decoder of what we have shared above, but listen with your bodily organs, especially your heart, spleen, liver, and gallbladder. What kind of emotions are you feeling? Then, find the logical explanation for your emotions and the words to express your feelings.

Since your alien mind is experiencing Earthly amnesia, reading the symbols, recognizing the signs, and looking at the colors as expressions of emotions is a safe way to remember your past. This way of teaching bridges your mind and heart, helping you create the heart-mind connection so you can access 5D memories. This work will set you on a journey to explore your ancient past and understand it from a slightly different angle.

Chapter 3

Ending The Cycle

The Space Ship
Maggie's Dream

"Your cycle is finished," said a voice. Maggie woke up instantly. She had heard this voice in her dreams before. Over the years, while searching for truths and learning to apply them to her spiritual growth, the voice became a normal part of life.

Today is the twelfth day of Christmas, and it's also my birthday, thought Maggie. Well, I don't feel like this is my last day on Earth, but maybe this is a sign that this could be my last lifetime on Earth? Does this mean I can finally ascend and go home? Maggie sighed.

"I will miss coffee, she thought dreamily. Can you imagine Maggie's Beings in the Pleiades or Sirius," she humored herself. Having a successful small franchise was her dream, but she struggled to keep just one store open for now.

The sun was rising on the horizon, and instead of waking up, she fell back to sleep and dreamt she was on her grandparent's farm. The house was exactly as she remembered when she was a child. Her grandparents were busy with their usual chores; she could even smell the fire in the wooden stove and sauerkraut soup cooking in the pot. Her heart swelled with happiness. Her grandparents passed away a while ago, but in her dreams, they were always alive. Somehow, Maggie knew this was her last visit. Their farmhouse was always a safe, rejuvenating place in her dreams. Over the years, it has become an escape from the demands of everyday life. Some people cannot sleep at night, and some cannot wait to fall asleep. Maggie loved to sleep.

"I know you love me," she whispered in her dream.

She walked outside the farmhouse she knew by heart in this lifetime, and her current reality morphed into a different place in a parallel life. Maggie felt comfortable traveling in her parallel lives and exploring strange new places through lucid dreaming. Everything happens for a reason, she thought.

The farm was still thriving, the animals were taken care of, and in this reality, they even had funny-looking beavers as farm animals.

"Dogs, I need to ensure the dogs are warm," she mumbled. She could not find the hay they usually put in their dog houses, but she found extra clothes that used to belong to her sister when she was young. It reminded her of how much she missed her. She carefully put them in the dog house. When she stood up, she could see the fruit orchards in front of her, and deep inside, she knew the farm was thriving. It was good to see it all one last time with such clarity.

Suddenly, Maggie moved in time and space again. Instead of the farm, she was standing on the shore of a lake or ocean; she was unsure. Confused, she tried to look around. She squinted her eyes and realized that something was wrong. She felt like she was drugged or poisoned, and it was spreading in her body. She intuitively knew she had to hurry before she lost consciousness. The bright sun added sensitivity to her eyes, and it was challenging to keep them open. She had a feeling that she was swelling as well. There were people she noticed, such as those who were suntanning, swimming, and vacationing, all looking healthy, except for her.

They have no idea, she thought. I have to hurry, they cannot leave without me!

Frantically, she ran into the water, feeling sicker with each passing second. Then, finally, she felt a glass surface under her feet. It was slowly sinking like a submarine.

If I don't do anything, they will leave without me. They cannot leave me here. "Wait for me!" she shouted, "Don't leave me here!"

She banged on what appeared to be a transparent glass platform with all her remaining strength. Some people close by saw her doing this and came to join her. They probably thought that she was just splashing for fun. No one wondered how strange or surreal it was to have this moving transparent platform under the water where they were swimming a minute ago.

Then, suddenly, a lid opened on the glass platform, and someone pulled Maggie inside.

Maggie knew she was in an underwater spaceship clouded by transparent technology, appearing like clear water to those around her. She was guided to join a group of humans who looked ill or had some physical or mental challenges. Maggie knew they were brought aboard to be test subjects. How do I know this? She thought. She knew and was not afraid; everything just made sense. Maggie had noticed that the humans were preparing for some orientation tour.

Maggie's physical condition was getting worse. "I am not like them," she grasped the arm of the young woman guiding her. "I am like you," Maggie said. Maggie's eyesight was progressively worsening, but she held onto her intuition, which had led her to this place.

Did the sun and Earth's atmosphere poison me? She wondered silently. Then she noticed a man talking to a group of humans.

Did he introduce himself as John? She was trying to listen as he lectured on something. Standing in the back, Maggie could not hear or see what he had written on the whiteboard. Her breath was becoming labored. She knew if someone or something did not come to her aid, her physical body would shut down very soon.

She turned to the women again, "I am not like them," she whispered in a desperate plea for help, her blue eyes begging for compassion.

"My name is Aria," said the woman, smiling kindly at Maggie. "Maybe you would like to have a smoothie?" she asked with an empathetic suggestion, "Kiwi?" she did not wait for Maggie's answer and continued, "Why don't you bring some avocado from the ice table? It's already sliced. I'll start this smoothie for you." With a kind smile, she thrust a small cup into Maggie's hand. Somehow, Maggie knew this woman should not be talking to her. She walked to a table with several ice containers with fresh fruit and vegetables pre-sliced to perfection.

Maggie found a spoon to scoop slices of avocado. She forcefully blinked her eyes to see better and realized that the coordination in her hands had also started to decline. Maggie instinctively knew that she was racing against time. She had to get to this avocado quickly. To her surprise, the avocado differed from the consistency she was familiar with—it had a slimy, jelly-like consistency. Her increasingly poor motor skills made it difficult to scoop. It took all her concentration and hand-eye coordination to accomplish this small task.

She handed it to Aria, who, in exchange, gave her a small cup with what looked like tiny orange fruits in a slimy sauce. She said, "You need to eat this." Maggie took the cup and looked hesitant at the weird, jelly-like substance. Somehow, she trusted this woman, as if she knew her, and had an intuitive feeling that this woman could get into trouble by helping her. "Eat it, eat it, "she urged her quietly.

Maggie tentatively tasted it. It looked weird, but it was pleasing to her senses. Aria went to make the smoothie.

After eating a cup of what appeared to be alien fruit, Maggie started to feel better. The swelling was going down, the confusion was clearing up, and a new shocking revelation entered her mind, "I belong with these people who are studying those people. Oh my God." Maggie felt cold, sweating in horror. "Who am I, and how do I know this?

Aria held her chin steady with one hand and looked directly into Maggie's eyes while speaking telepathically.

"We do not mean harm to them. We study them, especially their nervous system, and then safely return them home. The purpose of this study is to understand human evolution and to estimate a time when they can all graduate out of the quarantine of Earth and take their rightful place as planetary beings. We cannot just miraculously heal them or give them necessary knowledge, except a few select humans who will serve as examples of everything possible. There are some things we are allowed to do. We can show and teach them how to heal during our encounters with them, but they must incorporate it into their normal life and help themselves and others. The problem is that often, they are terrified when they remember. They automatically assume they have been abducted and experimented on in the most gruesome ways. Because they grew up with suggestive thinking that alien encounters are dangerous, quite often fear prevents them from utilizing what they have learned here."

Aria continued, "To assist them directly, we have to incarnate amongst them and become the Bringers of Knowledge, Masters of Healing, or the Minds of the Brave, and lead them to their graduation or, as you call it, ascension. Studying them helps us design a curriculum for those bright divine souls like you, Maggie, who volunteered to enter human incarnation to assist others. Each century poses different challenges. Therefore, the teachings need to be adjusted from time to time. The ancient truth is the same in any given period. It is just explained from a different point of view. As you already know, these volunteers have to face their own challenges that can turn into personal darkness upon awakening. Unfortunately, there is always some price to pay."

I got lost in living a human life, believing I am human like them, Maggie thought silently, knowing that what she heard was true. She did not realize that she was speaking telepathically to Aria and continued in her thoughts.

The Earth is a beautiful place, but for beings like us, extraterrestrial beings, it is a place that poisoned our minds. When our mind is clouded, our eyes are closed, our ears do not hear, and our hearts and souls are lost in the vast sea of human emotions. This happened to us in ancient days following the fall of Atlantis. We became fearful because we lost all control and became survivalists. Eventually, we entered human incarnations and became either victimized or angry. We found our own way to control our lives, Maggie recalled, as she was suddenly flooded with memories.

"Our need for control creates mental illness, makes our nervous system sick, and it is us who create the darkness in our life? Oh my gosh, is this why you study the nervous system?" Maggie shouted out loud.

"Shhh." Aria put her finger on her mouth, signaling for silent, telepathic communication. "You are starting to remember." She smiled at Maggie. "You are not trapped on Earth by your karma, but by your beliefs, which are programmed in your nervous system." She paused and looked directly into Maggie's eyes. "Maggie, remember when you wake up, remember our conversation, and remember your awakened lifetimes when you held your fifth-dimensional divine consciousness in your human physical three-dimensional body."

Maggie woke up, mumbling out loud, "My amnesia should clear now. I am done with my Earthly life cycles. I can return back home."

BEGINNING AND ENDINGS
Pleiadian Transmission

Every beginning has a predestined ending. Every journey has a final destination. A seed germinates, blossoms, and becomes a beautiful flower that eventually withers and dies. Every ending is a threshold to a new beginning; therefore, you must experience constant changes to reach this threshold. Since you are a microcosm of a macrocosm, you can see this law mirroring in the Earth and in the Universe. Life in this Universe is a constant flow of changes, some hardly noticeable and some like blossoming flowers, right before your nose for you to acknowledge. Earth is a beautiful teaching place. Look at the living life around you, plants, trees, animals, and humans – especially babies. Their life force (energy) constantly flows, and they change every second.

Changes cannot happen without necessary transformation from one part to another. You always have a choice on how to relate to this step. The transformation could be perceived as painful on an emotional or physical level, but it also could be meaningful, loving, joyful, and peaceful if understood intellectually. For example, the pain of childbirth rewards you with a new life, and often, memories of the pain disappear as soon as the mother holds her newborn baby. When pain, struggles, suffering, or obstacles have a divine purpose behind them, and you are aware of the reward they could bring, they are perceived very differently than those you cannot see the meaning of or when you are overtaken by fears. Mastering control of the mind over matter, having an intellectual understanding of what you are experiencing (from the records of ancient knowledge), trusting yourself, and not fearing the unseen realm have been practiced in Mystery School initiations since ancient times. Every beginning eventually changes to an ending, only for a new beginning to emerge. You can view this as a circular motion; however, if you consciously focus on transformation through your unavoidable change, the circle becomes a triangle, and you already know that the meaning of a triangle is a catalyst. You do not have to repeat the same mistakes or lifetimes on Earth.

Many of the ancient initiations are not for the faint of heart. You have to become a master of your mind and your soul and its emotions. To succeed in this, you have to:

1. Trust yourself

2. Have a strong belief in yourself, live your purpose (in your soul's mission)

3. Control your thoughts and be aware of the emotions they create (become a master of your seas)

4. Most importantly - YOU have to **become a doer** (physically practice what you have learned)

I AM A DOER
Sirian Transmission

Ancient knowledge is only helpful if it is practiced. The only reason to rekindle ancient knowledge is to share or teach it to others. And if you desire to be a True Teacher, you have to practice all you have intellectually learned. If you desire ascension, you have to share with others what you have learned, and what you have learned naturally becomes your way of life, not just part of your practice.

When you enter the dark night of the soul, you can wallow in self-pity or welcome the darkness. One who stands unafraid in the dark cave but refuses to move forward will never find the light of the new beginning, compared to the one who struggles but keeps moving forward. Fear can be transformed into confidence, an awareness of your surroundings, which you may need to survive in the outside world. Fear can freeze you or empower you. Ultimately, your personal beliefs will determine your success or failure.

YOUR BELIEF
Pleiadian Transmission

Your personal beliefs will determine how you will feel about the outcome of any situation. This applies to even the most extreme conditions. For example, you may have chosen to save someone's life at the cost of your own or well-being. If you intended to save a life, you have succeeded, no matter the consequences.

Now, we want you to take the last sentence and apply its knowledge to your past lives, all the way until the lifetime when you relocated from Atlantis to Egypt. You will find many lifetimes where you sacrificed your own life, even opportunities to ascend and save others. You cannot consciously remember all of this, so you are assuming that something went terribly wrong, that you failed because you are still here and have traumas from past lives.

You are not a failure, and it is time you change that belief about yourself. You are worthy, you are incredible, and thousands of years have gone by, and you are still striving to serve humanity. Humanity may have ups and downs, but it still thrives because of your kindness, not your failures.

Strong beliefs create reality. Now, it is up to all of you to determine the next course for the Earth and its inhabitants. Your beliefs, married to your feelings and carried out through your actions, create a new reality. You are much more powerful than you think. You are the creator. You are the reality writer. Your beliefs give the ink to your pen.

EARTH'S DIMENSION
Pleiadian Transmission

Many of you worry that the Earth is entering an apocalypse. Predictions of this kind, the extinction of humanity or the collapse of civilization, have been circulating for a long time, yet you are still here. The Earth is far away from ending her existence. It is the third planet from the sun and a three-dimensional living being. It will stay like that, but it supports life that can awaken to seven-dimensional energy and graduate from her school. The Earth is a library for various beings in the Universe, and it has been like this since we found it during Lemuria. Life comes and goes; some evolve, and some become extinct. The environment changes, the weather changes, the poles shift, and yet Earth is still the same three-dimensional being.

At this time, you are reaching fifth-dimensional energy, and Earth fully supports you through this. Human life was always meant to evolve and enter multi-planetary life. Some of you think Earth is changing its dimensional frequency with you, but that is misleading information.

What is currently changing is the energy of the inner Earth, the crystalline grid energy. The inner Earth is occupied by various ET life forms that hold different dimensional energy and support you. The crystalline grid is being programmed to support your evolution. Two thousand years ago, the Essenes activated the 4D energy in the crystalline grid to open the heart of humanity and set in motion the 5D energy that would open approximately two thousand years later and open the mind of humanity. None of this would have been possible if the Essenes did not work in union with the beings living in the inner Earth and the benevolent Cosmic begins that gathered for this spectacular event on Sirius A. See, since the beginning of a new life in Egypt, soul families have synchronized their incarnations so that they meet approximately every two thousand years to assist in the collective transformation of humankind, as well as their collective journey back home.

Remember, the Earth is a valuable training ground for everyone who would like to achieve multidimensional, planetary life and work toward complete ascension from this Universe.

At this present time, human life on Earth has come to a rare fork in the road that you only encounter every few thousand years, where time and light bend, where the past and the future meet in the present time so you can decide which road you will take. When you reach 5D, you can perceive reality, which is invisible to the untrained eye. You can see the past, and you can see possible futures. This could be scary or shocking to you at first. You may think that you are being controlled by AI programs, that you may have implants, or that you are being controlled by other beings, or that you have been part of the ET group that is knowledgeable about these things. Many of you may become angry and cannot pass over this realization.

You want to see the truth, but the truth is only sometimes pretty. This Universe is composed of two primary energies, male and female or, as you call it, Dark and Light. We like to call it mind and soul. These two energies have been competing for dominance for millions of years, only to discover that their union was their original task. Therefore, the first thing to do when perceiving 5D energy is consciously understanding the dysfunction and chaos we all have co-created.

In 3D energy, your mind is coated in amnesia, in the illusion that you can create a perfect life by siding with either Light or Dark. This amnesia keeps you in a place of suspended, fake happiness here on Earth, where you fear anything new or unseen. This is a natural energy on Earth, like an addictive drug. The Earth heightens our senses and clouds our minds like a cup of sweet wine. It is not evil. It is just seductive, addictive, over-protective, and loving. It will keep you safe, as your ego would, until eternity. But that eternity would be on Earth.

When you reach 5D energy, you will start detoxing your mind from Earthly 3D amnesia. You will have to be super careful with your emotions and thoughts, let go of your need to control the outcome of your actions, let go of your judgment, and become an observer for a while.

LAST INCARNATION
Pleiadian Transmission

Do you desire this to be your last incarnation? If yes, you have a good chance of accomplishing this step. What you have learned will always stay with you. What you have physically gathered in your lifetime or inherited from your ancestors will remain behind for others to enjoy. You do not need any physical riches or super magical objects on your new journey, as this journey is beyond the realm of Earth. What you need is a healed soul. This will be your last incarnation ONLY if you heal your soul. To heal your soul, you need ancient knowledge. To have ancient knowledge, you must share it with others while in service. It may seem like a never-ending circle, but it is absolutely achievable. A mother with a kind, loving heart never needs to work out of the house if she shares her mother's wisdom, love, and compassion with everyone who enters her life. She is in service to humanity. When someone touches your heart, it awakens the well full of feelings within you. A brilliant mind connected with a caring heart is what this world needs. While approaching her life with acceptance, forgiveness, and unconditional love for herself and others, she heals her soul, and when her time comes, she has a choice to say goodbye to a beautiful Earth. Your unselfish actions with a belief in yourself open the door to a new beginning.

The first part of the ascension is spiritual ascension. This means understanding your thoughts, emotions, actions, past and current. You are not trapped in this world by your karma or collective karmic debt. You are trapped by your beliefs that vary from century to century depending on how you are conditioned by your family, society, spiritual beliefs, etc. When you start understanding this, your job is to change the patterns of your life and then become a living example to your friends. You can speak thousands of beautiful words and share many parables, but those will remain empty if they are not woven into your everyday life. You have to be true to your words, your actions have to support them, and you have to be a living example that works. You do not have to be perfect, but you cannot teach something and say that it works for others and helps thousands except for you. This is defective advice; by sharing it, you manifest negative energy that will create obstacles for yourself.

Understanding yourself is like walking backward through your journey. Strive to remember who you are. Rekindle the fire within you. Can you connect the dots of your past lives? Can you understand all the drama you have been part of? Can you walk back and overcome the anger, frustration, and pain others caused you? Can you forgive yourself for not being perfect and maybe even causing the same?

Can you move through the heavy emotions gathered on your journeys through various times and look without any judgment to see how magnificent you have been? Can you see how many lives you have saved? Can you see how much you have helped? On more occasions, you have helped with your ancient wisdom than with a silver blade. Your creed is to save and protect life at all costs. You sacrifice yourself, your sanity, and your soul for those who need your help. You did not ask for a hefty fee. You asked that they pay it forward to those in need. You set the act of kindness in motion, still rotating steadily. Why can't I be in the presence of this grace, of this magnificent self, you ask? And we answer truthfully, look into your heavy emotions created from your beliefs. They serve as a heavy iron gate that separates you from the real you.

Wake up, The Children of Light! It's time to remember the glory and grace of your whole being. Deep within you lie the memories of lives forgotten. It is all written in your DNA. Drink the rainbow ambrosia from the challis, hidden in the Holy Grail. Drink deeply to cure your amnesia of the belief that you are just human beings originating from wombs of the Earth. The Earth is your Mother, and the Universe is your Cosmic Father. A mother sometimes overprotects her child from the outside world because she loves her child. It is hard to let go; deep inside, you also know this. It takes a lot of courage to let go and trust the outcome.

A new beginning is dawning on the human race. It is also a time for the guardians to be changed so those ready can go home.

LEAP OF FAITH
Maggie's Story

"You need a little bit more exposure," said Frankie cheerfully.

Maggie and Frankie have been friends since high school. Even though Frankie already had two children while Maggie was building her career, they have always been there for each other on good and bad days.

"I am doing all I can, including ads in local newspapers and occasional coupons. I even have this free lending library here." Maggie swept her hand toward the bookshelf in the corner of her cozy shop.

"Yeah, yeah," mumbled Frankie, "You should add a few of those steamy romance reads. I would sit here all day long and read, and you can even babysit my angels."

"Keep dreaming, Frankie," laughed Maggie.

"Many of those books on the shelf have priceless spiritual advice. You can drink your coffee, read a page or ten, and you will leave satisfied with caffeine circulating in your blood and a seed of wisdom in your mind, and if that seed germinates, it will change your life," said Maggie proudly.

Maggie prized herself on her book selection. Occasionally, books disappeared without her permission, but then other customers would bring in some books they were ready to give out, so Cosmic balance, as Maggie called it, was in place.

"Okay, you're right. I still cannot believe I sat here the whole afternoon and read "The Shift" by Dr. Wayne Dyer. That story gave me a totally new perspective on life. But I think you need to get more people hooked on your coffee. It's so good, and you make your own bean blend that you won't even share with me. You are like a local caffeine dealer around here. You should bag your beans and sell them by the pound.

"Frankie!" Maggie exclaimed, "A caffeine dealer? And, if I sell my beans, will people still come by to have a cup of coffee?" asked Maggie with a concerned tone.

"Of course, silly. People not only love your coffee, but also your hospitality. Everyone loves you, Maggie, especially the people you employ," she jokingly pointed to herself.

"But seriously, let's create your label and sell it on Amazon and Etsy," she said, giving Maggie a long look and deliberately pausing before continuing.

"The package will be the unique expression of this place and you. You know I took those art classes, and I am itching to make something more special than just crafts with my kids. Please let me," Frankie pleaded.

"You add your beans and get people addicted to the best coffee on Earth."

"Now you are exaggerating, Frankie."

"Nope. Ask George. George?"

"I am listening to you ladies," he answered from his table, "And I have to side with Frankie. Your coffee is magic in itself. It would probably wake up the dead," he winked at them.

"I do not know," Maggie said, sitting down. She looked around. She loved this place, but she hardly made ends meet every month. She did not have the money to invest in a project that might fail.

"Why do you look so worried?" asked Frankie.

"What if no one likes it? Do you know how many different coffees are out there? I will not even be able to compete in price. I cannot buy it in big bulk sizes."

"Maggie, look at me," said George, "You have to stop seeing yourself as a failure and see yourself as a successful, abundant business owner. You have to believe in yourself, young lady. Don't you read your own books here?"

"George, if you were younger, I would ditch my husband and run away with you," said Frankie quite seriously.

"Look, Maggie, I will design your bags. I promise you the artwork on them will be something that everyone will want to showcase in their kitchen instead of hiding them in the cupboard."

"Frankie, you know I cannot pay for that," said Maggie, a little ashamed.

"I am not asking for money. A little babysitting would definitely help, but I do not ask for money. You have always been there for me; now it is my turn to give back."

"Thank you," said Maggie.

George slowly got up. He was almost eighty, and his knees gave him troubles. "Time for me to pay for my coffee," he said as he handed Maggie his credit card.

"Credit card?" Maggie wondered. George, I know you like to pay with cash. You can pay me tomorrow. Please do not worry about it."

"Oh no, let's use this," he insisted. When Maggie gave him the small paper to sign his signature, he added a $3,000 tip. "Thank you, Maggie, for all you do," he handed it to her and started to walk away.

Maggie smiled and thought how fortunate she was to have such a loyal customer. When he was almost to the door, she looked at the receipt and froze.

"George?" she said slowly, "I think you made a mistake. Please let me correct this for you."

"It is not a mistake, Maggie. It is a donation to your success. When my wife passed away, I was lost. I thought I would never find happiness again. My wife loved coffee, and she would love this place. When I found it, your kindness touched my heart. You care about everyone who walks through these doors. Your book corner has filled me with hope for a new generation, and of course, your coffee bean selection is superb. I have done well for myself in life. I will not take any of my money with me after I die, and it could make a difference in someone else's life, so why not do it."

"I will pay you back, George," said Maggie

"No, I will not accept that, but I will ask you to pay it forward one day when you are successful and see someone else struggle." Then he opened the door, "I bid you a good day, ladies."

Maggie ran around the counter and hugged George, tears running down her face, "Thank you, George, thank you."

CHAPTER 4

TREES

MANIFESTATION
Maggie's Dream

Maggie was back in the city she grew up in, yet it looked slightly different than she remembered. She thought I must be in a lucid dream again and allowed herself to experience this fully.

A crowd of people was entering a building on Main Street. Intuitively, she knew it was a House of Prayer, and she wondered what the crowd meant. To whom or what are these people praying? Why are they doing what they are doing, and what do they receive? Somehow, she also knew you would have to pay for these services.

Curious, Maggie walked into the house. It felt like the whole city was coming to this place. What is so special about it, she thought. I am just going to have a quick look. And I am not going to become a sheep like these people, she assured herself mentally.

Inside, it looked like a community fair. Stations were set up in several areas of the room. Once you walk in, you have to keep moving in one direction. Suddenly, there were people in front of her and behind her. Maggie felt trapped.

"Excuse me," she said out loud, hoping to get attention without yelling. "Can I just go back through the entrance door?" When no one answered, she added apologetically, "I was just curious to see what it looks like here." Some people just looked at her without saying a word. Others just minded their own business.

She felt pushed toward the first station. "I am sorry. I would like to return. I was just..."

"Curious?" spoke a woman behind her.

"Yes," Maggie turned toward her.

"I just want to go back. This is not for me. But these people behind me would not move or make space for me to leave."

"How would you know this is not for you without trying?"

Maggie checked her jeans pocket, "I do not even have money to try. I'm not poor. I do have money, but it's just not here with me. I just have a few cents in my pocket. I feel bad about that. I need to leave."

"You will figure that out," the woman smiled quietly.

"There are three stations. At the first station, you state your wish, an intention, or, as we call it, a prayer for what you would like to receive. At the second station, you write it down and put it in the basket. You will know what to do when you reach the third station."

"Now, you have to keep moving, and I cannot talk to you from now on," the woman said in a kind voice.

Maggie felt frustrated but not afraid. If I had only brought some money with me, now it would look like I was just taking advantage of these people, she thought. What would they think? What would they do when they realized I could not pay them? At the moment, Maggie didn't think she could pay with a credit card, sign a check, or ask for a bill to pay later, as we often do in our everyday Earthly lives.

Everything is happening "now" in this city, and even paying your bill had to be done when the time came, without any excuses. She knew that, but how she knew, she had no clue. She just knew.

The woman nudged her toward a praying station. With a little shrug and a sigh, Maggie clasped her hands over her heart, closed her eyes, and made her wish in silence. At least I'll try. Then, someone nudged gently to write down her wish.

When she was done, she looked where the third station was but couldn't see anything.

Just then, the crowd directed her out of the back door into what appeared to be a backyard trail leading into the woods. All these people walked peacefully, in silence, on the trail. "Where are they going?" Maggie wondered out loud. Obviously, there was only one way, and no one was walking back. Like the Prayer House, there was only one way in, one flowing direction of traffic, and no one was walking back towards her. It seemed she was the only one concerned about this.

"I guess you get some exercise here, too," she said jokingly to the woman she met in the house.

The woman just raised her eyebrows without saying a word. Maggie translated this into, whaaat are you talking about? A few others gave her an odd look, as well.

"You know, like when you pay for a membership. So here you pray and have a good brisk walk through nature. You pray and exercise." She flashed her charming smile this time to win them over.

They just gave her an even weirder look and kept walking. Maggie felt like she might have annoyed them. Then, the woman pointed at the trees and made a facial expression so that she would notice them.

Trees, those are lovely trees, thought Maggie. She loved nature and realized she missed being in the forest. She missed the sound of the birds, the scent of the woods, and quiet, undisturbed places. These are lucky people, she thought, and from that moment, Maggie was deeply grateful she could walk with them toward the unknown. She felt peaceful, soothing, warm vibrations in her whole body and trusted that whatever the next station was would be fine. She liked the walk in the forest. She even enjoyed the company of these people who walked silently with her. She let go of her worries at that moment and felt like she could do anything. Then she saw a glimpse of the house on the hill and people gathering in front of it. The reality of her situation came back. She rubbed her jeans pocket; I would have felt much better if I had taken some money.

She looked at her left wrist and realized she wore her rose quartz bracelet. She rubbed her fingers over the pink beads. This bracelet always filled her with love. She remembered the note it came with: Rose quartz is a vessel of unconditional love. Its gentle energy guides you in fair giving and receiving unselfish love. Should I give it to them as payment? No, she thought this bracelet had such a deep meaning. Her mother bought it for her. She felt protective of her little treasure. She looked over her shoulder at the woman who had helped her before, but this time, she respected the code of silence and smiled politely at her. She took a deep breath and began to walk the last part of the hill towards the gorgeous mountain house with enormous futuristic glass windows.

Suddenly, she sensed the woman behind her. "Don't turn; keep walking, and just listen," the woman said quietly.

Maggie obeyed.

The woman quietly whispered, "I know you have a few coins in your pocket. You can feel them and know for sure they are there. Take a deep breath in and physically feel them. Now move your hand and rest it over your pocket."

Maggie did it.

"Empty your mind and focus on the seed of light in your heart. Your seed is like a seed of these trees. Just breathe in and out the essence of these trees until you are one with them. Know and feel that with every cell in your body, there is also a $20 bill in your pocket. Nothing is impossible if you truly believe."

Puzzled, Maggie kept her hand over the pocket. Could she really manifest something by just believing and thinking about it? Could she make a $20 bill appear in her pocket?

She looked around her, observing the magnificent trees that stood there for hundreds, maybe even thousands of years. The scent of the forest, especially the pine trees, began awakening some distant memories within her.

Why not believe? What do I have to lose, she thought, and followed this woman's advice. She put her hand over her jeans pocket, and for that moment, she fully believed she had a $20 bill. At the same time, she felt her body's vibrations. Every cell in her was buzzing like a beehive. Once she let go of her analytical mind and visualized that there was a seed of a tree in her heart, she felt as if she transformed into a birch tree. The birch tree became one with the trees around her. She felt incredible. Time she has ceased to exist for a moment. All the stress and anxiety she felt was gone. It was just the forest, and she was one with it on a soul and cellular level. It felt incredible to be one with nature. She was as old as the first tree on the Earth. She could feel the roots of the trees reaching from one to another, as a friend would give you a hand in need. At one moment, she was a young seedling in the Earth's rich soil; the next, she was a tree a few hundred years old, bent down by the weight of its branches. She was everything, and in that split second, she understood the whole evolution of Earth.

Just then, someone nudged her, and she realized she was in front of the glass door of a futuristic house. The woman walking with her opened a door and motioned for her to enter.

"You are not going in?" Maggie asked, perplexed.

The woman smiled and shook her head in silence. She waved, urging Maggie to go on. The door closed behind Maggie, and she found herself in a long hallway; at the end, she could see three entrances. The first two had people waiting in line. She looked over her shoulder toward the glass door and was happy to see the women with others visibly cheering for her, signaling with their hands—not that door, the next one, keep going.

Curiously, she reached into her pocket and found a crisp $20 bill there. Trying to hide the shock on her face, she rubbed it between her fingers to see if it was real. Did I really put it there? Did this happen? she pondered. With a questioning look, she looked over her shoulder towards the people outside. They were cheering for her.

What an odd place! They wouldn't talk to me, but now they are cheering for me, she thought, puzzled. She kept walking past the lines of people toward the last door. There was no one standing in that line.

"The Council," the sign on the door read. She took a deep breath before she knocked on the door and woke up in her bed.

SEED OF LIGHT
Pleiadian Transmission

YOU are a divine being traveling through various constellations in this Universe. Every time you encourage yourself to experience life on a different planet, whether Light or Dark in nature, you have an incarnation there. Your seed of light finds a supportive environment, and it germinates. This seed will start growing into a tree (metaphorically said), the tree of your life, and it will learn how to adjust to the environment and survive. You will experience many lessons, some easy and some rather challenging. You may experience power struggles between the soul and the mind. Your task is to find the knowledge of how to solve this, learn from it, and find wisdom in every experience. When you mature, you are supposed to share your knowledge. Every tree has the potential to share its seeds, which are illuminated with the light of knowledge for future generations to learn from. Your inner light has the power to generate light for others to find. This light could be hidden within the seed, sometimes even for thousands of years until it finds the right environment to germinate.

Trees on the Earth are symbols of the Universal Tree of Life. You are the seed of the Universal tree, a seed of light that carried all the knowledge of the Universe to Earth. Due to traumatic events that you have experienced in several lifetimes, you have forgotten about this light within you, and you keep searching for knowledge outside of you instead of searching within your tree of life. Once your seed remembers its light, it will guide you to higher spiritual knowledge.

Each of you has the potential to access ancient knowledge, and when you do, you need to keep the cycle going. Out of knowledge, wisdom is born. Wisdom can only be found by actively practicing your knowledge, not just by dreaming about it. You learn what works and does not work for you in any lifetime. Each life is very different, which is why you have been many trees throughout your incarnations.

When you find yourself at a roadblock, see it as a tree that has fallen over on your path. Instead of blaming and complaining, stop for a while, rest, and honor the life force of the fallen tree so you can make this stop. Review your life and ask questions to help you find the answers. Instead of asking, "Why am I not receiving more knowledge, guidance, and miraculous healings?" ask, "What am I not doing? What is it that I am not seeing? What is it that I am not hearing?" And if you still do not know, focus on others instead of your problems. A selfless act of kindness goes a long way and always returns in many unexpected ways.

Physical manifestation is achieved when your mind and heart communicate (we discussed this principle in detail in PC2). Mastering the magic of manifestation may sound exciting and like an answer to your problems, but there is more than the eye can see. In the world of duality, even the art of manifestation has to obey the rule of twos. When you receive, you need to give. When you give, you need to allow yourself to receive. What you will give, you will receive. This creates harmony and balance. It is the basic principle, which is very simple and has been taught since ancient days. It applies to both physical and spiritual manifestations.

Maggie manifested her $20 bill, which she then paid to the Council, not because they needed physical currency, but as a symbol of giving and receiving. It is a cycle that requires active movement to benefit from. When Maggie walked behind the door of the Council, she instantly recognized familiar faces, and it was evident that physical possessions last only one lifetime. The amount in your bank account had no meaning there. She also realized that what kind of person you are in your heart matters and that the soul's knowledge, even though temporarily blocked, is everlasting and a true treasure. No one told her that. She remembered all of this while she was connected to the library of trees, located on the fourth floor at the Temple of her body. What Maggie received behind the doors of the Council was of much more value than any physical possession, and Maggie received this so she could share this gift with all of you.

SEED OF LIGHT MEDITATION
Recommended to do outside

1. Take a deep breath in and release all the air out.
2. Take another deep breath and exhale all the worries and expectations.
3. Say aloud or in your mind, "I ask and thank you for connecting with the highest available energy of God, my higher self, and the frequency of unconditional love."
4. Rest your hands over your heart chakra, pressing gently at your sternum, and feel the seed of light within you. This is where your soul and mind connect to your nervous system. Your journey begins here.
5. Now imagine that you are a tree, your tree of life. Be any tree you would like to be.
6. Your feet grow the roots that anchor you deeply into Mother Earth. You are safe and supported. These roots hold the stories of all your past lives on Earth.

7. Your body becomes the trunk of your tree, with all of your present life encoded there. This is your headquarters, your navigation center.

8. Your arms, neck, and head become the mighty crown of your tree, connecting you to the Universe and your family of light. What a magnificent tree you are.

9. Breathe in deeply the energy from the Earth - for three counts - through your roots, your tree trunk, and your heart chakra. Hold your breath there for three counts, and breathe it out to the Universe through the crown of your tree for three counts.

10. For three counts, breathe in deeply the energy from the Universe through the crown of your tree into your heart chakra. Hold your breath for three counts, and breathe it out into the Earth through your roots for three counts.

11. Repeat steps 9 and 10 two more times.

12. Now, bring your focus into your heart chakra. Stay present and focus on your breath. Let go of everything and connect to nature and the other trees around you. Be one with the trees closest to you. Feel that your heartbeats are one. Close your eyes and feel the Earth below your feet, feel the Universe above your head, and feel connected to both simultaneously. Feel the light within you dancing to your heartbeat.

13. When you feel done, become aware of your entire body and express your gratitude to everyone, "Thank you, thank you, thank you."

When you are one with nature, you are one with the invisible fourth-dimensional energy, which is the secret of feeling. Ancient knowledge has been hidden within the etheric energy for safekeeping, as it is an invisible field to the untrained eye. To access this knowledge, you need to enter the fourth-dimensional energy. The seed of light in the trunk of your tree of life is a doorway, and unconditional love is the key that will open that heavily guarded door. When you work with the meditation above, imagine walking out through your heart and into the world of nature's fourth-dimensional energy. Enjoy this magical world. Have fun, and always close the door behind you when returning.

DREAMS
Lights of the Universe Transmission

Dreams are an easier way for us to communicate, interact with, and teach you in 5D energy. Consider it a modern-day Mystery school, where your ancient elders are the ones who invite you to the program when you are ready. While you are in a deep sleep, your soul travels into the higher dimensions, and for us, it is the easiest time to connect with you, especially through your lucid dreams, as this is when your ego is not sabotaging you.

We suggest that you start keeping a dream journal. You can train yourself to recall your dreams. Upon awakening, bring yourself into the present time, your left hand on your bladder and your right hand on your forehead, and in your mind, drift back into the story of your dream to remember it all. It may take a little practice, but with perseverance, you will become efficient in recalling your dreams. You will notice that we hardly talk to you in your dreams, as that is against the rules, but you will also notice that we can teach you through the stories you experience. Pay attention to all the signs, symbols, and meanings. Do not dismiss a bad dream as an undesirable nightmare; question what I could have learned from this. Your dreams are a safe place to try various scenarios without bringing harm to your physical life. Everything is possible, and you will not die from bad choices. Therefore, once you know that you are in a dream, you can train yourself to be emotionally neutral in that place. Observe any situation without having to be a hero or a victim. You can become an active part of your dreams with some practice.

Ask yourself questions:
-   How can I help assist myself in having the life I desire in that dream?
-   What kind of beliefs do I need to transform?
-   How can I help people in my dreams without harming others?

- How can I use my creative power without causing chaos?
- If I change my life or alter the life of the whole city or nation in my dream, what kind of domino effect will I create?

Dreams are such a powerful teaching tool in the Mystery School. Bring what you have learned in these lessons into your waking life. Observe your life and how these signs, symbols, and even parallel stories of your dream show up throughout your day. When you acknowledge it, you create resonant energy, and more will come.

Observe and journal:
- How did my dream reflect something I am trying to master?
- Do I see the gentle guidance weaving into my daily life?

The more you stay neutral and pay attention to small details, the more you will notice that you are not alone and that guidance is always there. You will also notice that what you master in your dreams will be positively reflected in your everyday life. You are gently learning to apply 5D energy from your dreams to your 3D everyday life. The purpose of being in the Mystery School in your dream state is to gain knowledge and skills to share with others.

You are a light of the Universe; within you is a seed of light. The knowledge from the Universal Tree of Life is within your seed, and while you are living on the

Earth, you are a light of the Earth, a child of oneness, bringing hope for the future.

CHAPTER 5

INTERDIMENSIONAL COMMUNICATION

AIRPORT

Mikael's Dream

Mikael walked through the long halls of the airport. He was dressed casually in black, with earbuds in his ears, and his tall, athletic body moved with determination. His emerald green eyes scanned his boarding ticket: Constellation Orion, Planet Mintaka. It felt normal. The anticipation of returning back home quickened his pulse. He checked his watch for the time and realized that it looked different from the Apple watch he usually wore. The display seemed to be under his skin or part of his forearm, like an implant, and instead of numbers and words, there were symbols, symbols he understood. Suddenly, his eyes started losing focus, and his sharp mind clouded as an unexpected, annoyingly loud sound came out of nowhere. Mikael opened his eyes and realized he was dreaming and was in his bed in New York City.

Annoyed, he shouted, "Alexa, stop!" He sat up in his bed and shook his head, Orion? It felt like he was really there.

ET UNIVERSITY
Maggie's Dream

Maggie dreamed that she was returning to school in a strange city. She dreamt of living in this city alongside extraterrestrial families on several occasions. They liked and accepted her, but being human was not equal here.

Our destructive emotional impulses are the problem, she thought. Maggie often watched positioned satellites in the sky; there were so many for various purposes, and they all looked like bright stars. They could move, align, and create exciting designs in the sky. If she were to break any of the rules in this city, she knew that the satellite technology could easily detect her. She had seen this before, the complete destruction of life from laser weapons positioned on satellites. How they could detect me, she wondered. Do I have any GPS devices inside of me?

When Maggie first started coming to this city, there were times when "they" tried to eliminate her. She didn't even know who "they" were or why they targeted her. Satellites would locate her and shoot deadly lasers at her. Interestingly enough, she was always helped by one or another of the extraterrestrial beings living there. They were similar in appearance to humans, and even though they never took her under their protection or taught her, they always gave her excellent advice.

Maggie found herself in her dorm at the University in this ET city. She smiled and thought this place resembled the castle from the Harry Potter movies.

"Hi, Maggie," a young woman walked into her dorm room.

How does she know my name? She does look somewhat familiar, thought Maggie, with a confused look on her face.

"Did you already pick your classes?"

"No," answered Maggie, looking at this girl and trying to remember where she knew her from.

"Here are a few from my list: ET Communications, ET Science, ET Technology, ET Society. There are so many to pick from," said the girl cheerfully.

"ET Communications?" I like that. Maggie was starting to feel excited. Maybe she will finally be accepted in this alien city. She liked it here. It was a fascinating place filled with intriguing people.

Maggie thought about a handsome guy with striking emerald green eyes she had met earlier. She couldn't remember what he looked like, just his eyes. Oh, those eyes... How could she forget those? Maggie turned her attention back to the girl again. Where do I know her from? Maggie wondered. Then it hit her. "Aria?"

Maggie woke up from her dream, but this time, she was excited. *I think they finally agreed to teach me! Whatever it brings,* she thought, *everything will be okay.* And with a beaming smile, she was ready for the day.

ALIEN FRAGMENT
Orion Transmission

You have an alien fragment within you that can assist you in connecting your 3D human mind to the 5D alien mind, allowing you to communicate with other dimensional beings. We know you will automatically think that you have an internal implant like Mikael or that it is an external ability you can only learn at school, like Maggie. It is neither one nor the other, yet the fragment is part of you.

Mikael remembers advanced ET technology, and Maggie will learn that all she is looking for is already within her. This alien fragment is part of your sleeping DNA. It does not automatically activate upon your awakening or DNA activation; it activates when you reach a specific frequency in your spiritual growth.

This fragment is not your soul, even though it resides within your soul for safekeeping, and it is not your mind, even though it is connected to your mind and can connect your mind to the Knowledge Keepers and ETs. It is a higher vibrational frequency, starting at 5D, that has to be mastered to be sustained in the 3D body. We will refer to this as an alien fragment for your enjoyment, but remember that one thing can have many names.

The alien fragment shall not be confused with the energy of the Tree of Life that the Pleiadians spoke about in the previous chapter. Every being on Earth has a seed of light, but not everyone has an alien fragment. Only the souls who experienced ET incarnations on different planets before arriving on Earth possess this energy.

Before you arrived on Earth in your alien body, you had training in the Pleiades on soul science and soul healing and in Orion on mind science and mind balance. These constellations were specially picked for training by the Council of Light and Council of Dark in Sirius A. You actively learned to use your alien fragment there. This training was adequate for the Lemurian project and the beginning of Atlantis. Then, with the influx of alien beings coming to Earth, many rules have loosened, yet some energy training was still treasured by wise souls, in the same way an old book filled with wisdom would be. Memories of this training are encoded in your DNA and may resurface in your dreams.

The alien fragment can stay dormant for hundreds if not thousands of years, but when it becomes active, you will definitely notice it when you reach a higher frequency. Everything is subject to the law of action and reaction, and on Earth, spiritual mirrors are everywhere in your life. When your fragment activates, on outside, you often experience some technically-based malfunctions to get your attention. You may find that electronics around you, like your phone, computer, washing machine, car, and other devices, will suddenly stop working or start acting up with weird glitches that come and go. Pay attention to which part actually breaks. It is often electronics, which represents your nervous system. On inside, you will experience extreme sensitivity, overwhelming your five basic senses. This is where you need to soothe and tune up your nervous system. These glitches indicate that something in your body requires attention (nervous system)so your alien fragment can start working properly.

Often, your nervous system needs upgrading because you are now ready to work with your higher-energetic alien nervous system. Think of your nervous system as an electrical system that needs to be upgraded to accommodate gadgets with higher voltage. This is a good sign, and what you are experiencing is normal.

ALIEN COMPASS
Pleiadian Transmission

The function of the alien fragment is to be your compass before it is upgraded to "walky-talky" radio frequencies. The first lesson in ET communication is to learn navigation techniques and to follow the compass within you. As birds and fish have their inner navigation system and compass to guide them during migration, you have yours. Before you learn to communicate, you must learn to listen. This is what the compass is supposed to teach you.

Your alien compass can be felt in your fourth chakra. You may experience it as a little fluttering sensation or gentle vibrations in your chest. Some people can feel the energy moving vertically up and down, or even pain. It is often mistaken for negative implants. When the movement becomes active, it may initially feel odd and uncomfortable. When you feel the fluttering or vibrations, notice what you were thinking or doing at that moment. Your alien compass is connected to that particular thought or action you were just experiencing. What was it? Try to remember. The fluttering is your affirmation that you are doing the right thing at the right moment. It is your guidance system. When you notice it, acknowledge it. It is active only as a compass, not as a warning device. When you are doing the wrong thing, it just lies dormant.

Eva's note: Some of you can already feel this alien fragment within you. When the movement becomes active, it may feel strange. One may even confuse it as a health issue. Use your own common sense and check with your doctor to stay healthy. This fragment will not make you sick. It may feel odd before you get used to working with it. If you are confident you are not experiencing medical issues but actual energy sensations, start paying attention to them. In my experience, it is always something positive, and the compass points me in the right direction of my work or personal endeavor. I often sense this when I make a soul-to-soul connection, and the other soul is ready for healing.

Your conscious training will begin once you become aware of your alien compass. Patience is a virtue here, and your practice will focus on consciously recognizing your emotions and feelings. The fourth chakra is 4D energy, which opens the door into an invisible realm of emotions and corresponding vibrations. Some Knowledge Keepers were secretly placed in a 4D field for safekeeping. Your alien compass reads your emotions and communicates with you through vibrations. It needs to be noted and acknowledged when it guides you. That's how you calibrate it to your needs.

The goal is that you will be consciously communicating in/with 4D energy. Therefore, after you master your personal emotional language, you can communicate with nature, animals, and Earth elements. If you can understand your emotions and what they tell you, you will also appreciate them.

Learning how to use your alien compass will guide you to the alien mind you used to have.

4D AND THE THREE STAGES AND BKROKENNESS
Pleiadian Transmission

When you reach the frequency of your alien fragment, you will experience three stages. You may already have experienced them several times in your life. Once you consciously recognize them, understand them, and apply the recommended suggestions for transformative healing, you will stop repeating them. This is where the true magic begins: when you open the door to 4D and become conscious of your alien compass. Many came to the sun of the Universe, but only a few found the courage to walk through the fire.

The three stages and the recommended suggestions for transformation and healing:

1. Broken Nervous System = Broken Beliefs
Throughout your life, you experience different kinds of shocks that may break you down, emotionally or physically. Perhaps the loss of a job, money, a loved one, the end of friendship, abuse, etc. This brought on a conscious awakening and questioning of your beliefs. Your suffering may induce a deep longing to know who

you are, why this is happening to you, and the need for change in your life.

When you are going through these experiences, your heart is hurt, and you may be feeling like you are having a nervous breakdown, or maybe you have already had one. You may feel overwhelmed, frustrated, angry, victimized, etc. You are most likely experiencing huge ups and downs; your life may be falling apart, and you may question the meaning of your life. When you start asking, you eventually begin to feel that your life needs a new direction, and at that point, you may notice that your compass is giving you directions. This is a good moment. You can start learning to recognize the feelings associated with the compass navigation and work on believing in yourself to become your healer and guru instead of relying on others to fix you. Your compass corresponds to positive feelings that should help you move forward.

Healing suggestions:
- Recognition of the human ego
- Transformation of the human ego into the universal intelligent mind (moving from lower vibration energy into higher vibration energy)
- Unity of heart and mind
- Unconditional love

2. Broken Body = Broken Connection to Earth

Once you find your new direction, you could experience issues with your body, such as food allergies, minor aches and pains, or other physical problems. Life-threatening illnesses are rare but also possible if you are a healer and need to learn energy healing. Your compass can be very active at this point, and if you pay attention, it can guide you toward a healthy body transformation. You will gain a healthy appreciation for your body and life on Earth.

Healing suggestions:
- Recognition of the body as a vessel for the soul and the ego/mind
- Changing habits such as lifestyle, diet, exercise, etc.
- Love for the body and development of crystalline body
- Learning and practicing any form of energetic self-healing

3. Broken Heart = Broken Connection to Yourself

This is the last but often the most painful step intended to fully activate your heart chakra and open your alien fragment. You all work too hard to protect yourself from your emotions because they hurt. Therefore, you may experience some life events that make you feel like your heart is being ripped apart with sadness, frustration, and maybe even anger.

A broken heart, as dreadful as it feels, is a doorway to understanding your raw, deep feelings of emotional darkness that go back to ancient times. These feelings are so potent that they can consume you for the rest of your life. A broken heart allows the ego to fill the mind with hate, anger, jealousy, withdrawal, etc. These low vibrational thoughts create corresponding feelings. If you are a star-seed, these feelings have ancient origins. You need to start embracing them instead of denying them. Become an expert in defining and accepting what you are thinking and feeling. Find the opposite side (a higher vibrational one) and hold it in your body until it becomes second nature.

Remember, you are living in a place where duality is experienced to its fullness. Every feeling, thought, and action is subject to two energy poles, positive and negative.

When you process your own emotions from this lifetime, you may experience a feeling of ancient sadness with no concrete roots you can identify. This is a very temporary feeling, but necessary. Your soul has been harboring so much pain over thousands of years, and you are ready to release that pain.

You may have been working well with your alien compass until now, but suddenly, your compass may feel broken, and you may feel stuck on Earth with no support from your spirit guides. During this process, you are feeling the agony of your emotions, and you may want someone to save you and take all these feelings away, but no one can do the work for you as you are becoming the master of your energy. If you want your compass to work, you must accept yourself and your past. Find forgiveness with yourself and others for any wrong-doings, and start with a clean slate instead of running or hiding from your heart. This is the way to heal and find the 4D vibration that will fully activate your compass and open the doorway to the dimensions of magic, where you will learn that behind every magical experience, there is a logical explanation.

Healing suggestions:
-   Conscious recognition of suffering energy, intense desire for change, honor your feelings
-   Stop looking for answers outside and walk into your darkness so you can understand it
-   Finding happiness in the small things of everyday life, learn to hold the vibration of that feeling
-   Appreciation of life, body, and Earth
-   Seed of Light meditation

FINDING HAPPINESS
Pleiadian Transmission

Your life may be busy, with your time divided between your family, work, and being in service to others. The more you are doing, the less time you have for yourself. You may have learned to be content, but do you remember how to be happy? Do you remember how to be a happy human on Earth? Happiness is not just a feeling; it has various vibrations. It is a slightly different vibration than the happiness you knew before your awakening. Observing the feelings and vibration of 3D ego-based happiness, 4D heart-based happiness, and 5D heart-mind-based happiness will be a good practice.

Finding happiness in small things in everyday life is heart-based happiness (4D). It is energy that your compass needs for its function. When your alien fragment connects, one of the functions is that you will be able to deeply connect with your star soul family in the Universe and in the Inner Earth. When that happens, you may experience an extreme longing to go home. You may remember your life in the Pleiades or another star system and become very sad and nostalgic. Because of this other-worldly experience, you may lose interest in your human life since your life is far away from those memories. Your current life may turn into more immense suffering because there is no fast button to exit it without automatically returning.

You will be able to experience other dimensions, and it could feel as real as your current life. Still, this experience is ONLY in your mind or in your lucid dreams or astral travels, which could be consciously induced, and yet you have to be able to be active and happy in your everyday, 3D life. You have to have balance in your thoughts, feelings, and actions. If you spend significant time in the astral plane otherwise you will start disconnecting yourself from everyday life's needs, failing to implement the energy from out there to the earthly life around you.

Finding happiness makes your life on Earth more enjoyable. Happiness is a choice. 4D happiness, if chosen, is bliss.

YOU ARE YOUR GUIDE
Sirian Transmission

The alien fragment is part of your own unique energy. It is not guidance from your soul group or any divine or celestial being in the Universe. When you want to be a 5D being, you must learn to take responsibility for your thoughts, emotions, and actions and apply them equally to improve your life and others. This is your little helper along your journey. You will feel it when you are moving in the right direction; when you are not, you may feel very stuck. You have entered a higher vibrational energy and need to keep your momentum up.

What is the reason for having this fragment? The answer is simple: share the ancient knowledge and find your way home.

Your alien compass will now guide you in the fourth-dimensional energy invisible to untrained human eyes. Those on the Path of the Light must understand the Path of Dark (the path of the mind). And those on the Path of Dark must understand the Path of Light (the path of the soul). This starts you on a new journey where you will learn about unity and wholeness, about Dark and Light energies that cannot exist one without the other.

CHAPTER 6

HELLO DARKNESS

STRUGGLING EGO
Sirian Transmission

When your alien fragment activates, and you start consciously using your alien compass, it will eventually trigger your human ego. The reason is simple: Your alien compass will send electrical signals to your 5D mind and initiate a connection. The purpose of the alien compass is to connect the heart and mind and open the pathways between them that you, yourself, disconnected during ancient times to keep the knowledge within the alien mind safe and inaccessible until you become fully awakened. Gaining access to your alien mind before awakening would be like opening "Pandora's Box" and letting out things humans are not ready for.

The knowledge we are sharing and the examples woven into Maggie and Mikael's story will help you understand your growing pains and why you may have set up all these blockages for yourself. Fear feeds off of the unknown. Be brave to seek the truth.

When darkness descends on you, it is not meant for you to get lost, but you will find that there is always a reason for it. Once your ancient amnesia starts clearing, you start fluctuating between 3D, 4D, and 5D energy. You will get glimpses behind the veil and see the darkness at its finest. You will also know the truth from the past and perhaps even memories from Galactic Wars. Darkness is just a place where Light is hidden. As with anything else, it is just energy. Only you can choose what it becomes for you. Within the darkness also rests the power that you have hidden for yourself. Not a physical tool but spiritual power (knowledge). This power is like a two-edged sword, so naturally, it is exceptionally protected until you fully understand its potential.

On a physical level, you may notice sporadic electrical surges, vibrations, ticks, or numbness throughout your body. Some may be a little uncomfortable, but this is only temporary. These symptoms may be synchronized with weird glitches in your electronic devices. Start paying attention to what is happening and what you are thinking and doing at that moment. This is your clue as to what you need to work out personally. You are ready for the next energy upgrade, which signifies that your nervous system can use more nourishment to sustain you through these changes. That is your task. Remember, the nervous system is your strength, powerhouse, doorway to your abilities, and antenna to the other worlds.

On an emotional level, your ego can plunge you into the deepest darkness of your emotions, and it will even take it up a notch to torture you on an intellectual level. This is not a dark night of the soul and may feel like a strong psychic attack. You may feel overwhelmed, tired, and moody and start procrastinating and sabotaging any of your endeavors that will help you move forward. As unidentified darkness sets in, it feels as if you will never see a clear sky again. This energy needs to be understood instead of being cleared.

BRIDGE TO THE MIND
Pleiadian Transmission

Your intelligent alien mind is trapped between the lower 3D ego and the higher 5D mind in the human body. To access the alien mind, you must transmute one into the other. Remember, the ego's sole purpose is to protect you by any means. The ego has a hard job that is not appreciated. The ego cannot be wiped out, locked in a cage, or banished; it has to be understood and transmuted, and for that, it needs to first feel safe and secure. You can use the principle "as above, so below" to create a safe bridge to connect them.

As Above so, Below

The body is a microcosm of a macrocosm. Everything has its opposite, no matter how big, small, significant, or insignificant. Your alien body (that you used to have) may be seen as the body "above" while your human body is "below". Alien bodies have a robust nervous system. Since human bodies were created with the DNA of the aliens, the human bodies have the capability of producing that same strong nervous system.

Let's apply the "as above, so below" principle directly to our bodies. You can separate the body's energy into three parts.

Lower three chakras (Earth life, past lives, ego,3D)
Heart chakra (Cosmic life, future, soul, 4D)
Upper three chakras (Earth life, present time, universal mind, 5D)

In the Universe of your own body, the lower three chakras are your "below," the upper three chakras are your "above," and the middle fourth chakra is the sun, the center of your Universe.

You are familiar with the term "gut feeling." It is a skill your human ego develops to protect you from danger or making mistakes. Your gut–inner intuition could be honed into perfection, but it is a 3D skill, an excellent skill that helps you to survive if you consciously listen to it. For explanation, we will call this "your below" skill in the body. Intellectually, if you have the "gut feelings" skill below (3D), then you must have a corresponding skill above within your 5D mind, which we call the "alien mind."

Taking a shortcut and jumping from 3D to 5D is not advisable without adjusting in 4D. Shortcuts will only lead to a backlash of negative consequences.

You already know that within your body, the heart chakra represents 4D energy. Within the heart chakra is the dimension of emotion and vibration that you need to master before you can communicate with the aliens that you dream about. Listen to your compass, which will show you and direct you to the answers that activate your 5D walky-talky.

You already know this phenomenal journey starts from 3D to 4D energy. Small steps will yield powerful strides. It is good to spend some time in 4D energy. It will allow you to become the master of your emotions, not its slave. Once you start consciously entering the 4D realm, it may feel like you have walked into a closed, dark, scary room. You may even feel frightened, but with some practice, you can work on transmuting your emotions, thoughts, and actions and learn how to apply the correct vibrational rate to the corresponding energies. Low vibrations are transmuted into high vibrations. Sadness into happiness, fear into courage, hate into love, etc.

Explore all three parts of your bridge. What kind of thoughts do you have "below"? Do they serve you in the best possible way? If they are low vibrational thoughts, what is the opposite of those thoughts?

What kind of feelings, what kind of emotions do you hold in "the center of your universe"? Do the thoughts from "below" affect how you feel in your heart? Do they cloud your sun?

If the answer is yes, how would it feel in "the center of your Universe" if you held the vibration of the opposite of those thoughts in your heart and gently exchanged old thoughts with new ones?

Then, explore your "above" center. How do your thoughts "below" affect the thoughts "above"?

For example, feeling unsafe in your first chakra will reflect a fear of trust in yourself and others in your seventh chakra. Your heart chakra could experience emotions of unhappiness, hopelessness, or anxiety every time you are not feeling safe.

Practice transmuting your lower-vibrational thoughts and emotions into higher ones. Feel the vibration of new thoughts or emotions in your heart chakra, and teach your body to hold this new frequency.

Transmuting your emotional thoughts from lower to higher is like walking on a balancing beam from one side to the other. Remember to stop in the middle, observe and learn.

TRUST

Pleiadian Transmission

In the previous chapter, we spoke of holding the vibration of happiness in your fourth chakra; now, add the vibration of trusting yourself to it. Trust is the logical thought in something that you can do. Believing in yourself is trusting that you will accomplish a set goal. Trust is based on knowing what you are doing.

If you have never learned to swim but trust yourself to plunge into deep water and begin swimming, you will find that this is a careless endeavor, and you risk drowning. But if you trust that you can learn to swim and take classes with a qualified instructor, this trust in yourself will help you learn to swim. This is the true meaning of trust. You must learn to trust and believe in yourself, knowing and trusting what you are doing along your path.

CHAPTER 7

THE GREEN STONE

IN THE MOUNTAINS
Mikael's Dream and Life

Mikael was in the mountain village again. How many times have I been to this place? Mikael wondered to himself in his dream.

The tiny village was snuggled in Mother Nature's protective arms, with mountains as a backdrop to the west and a nearby forest. He felt good, safe, and like he could live here forever, yet he knew he was only visiting. Every time he came here, he was a visitor, not like someone enjoying a vacation but someone patiently waiting for something, something he did not know how to explain.

This searching or waiting was very different from his life in New York City, where he was an expert in financial investments and managed portfolios for some impressive clients. His life was stressful and busy, but that is what he had chosen, and he had to remind himself that this is what he liked to do. "What would I do in a mountain village?" he wondered out loud. He did like the solitude of this place, the scent of the forest, and the gentle vibrations through his body that made him feel alive with a different desire than just being a financial expert.

"This place," he muttered in his sleep.

He noticed a group of people on a guided tour of this place. "Wouldn't it be easy to be just like them?" he thought.

"Excuse me, do you know where the bathroom is?" a woman wearing a long coat asked as she approached him.

"Walk that way down the street, and you will see it on the left," he said, pointing his finger.

"Thank you," she smiled and left.

She looks familiar, he thought briefly.

Mikael continued walking and was about to turn towards the nature trail when he noticed a car parked on the side of the road. In the backseat sat a girl, about 6 years old. Her long, dark blond hair curled on the ends, gently touching her shoulders. She opened the door and looked at him with what appeared to be the whole galaxy in her eyes.

"Are you okay? Can I help you?" he asked, as he noticed that her legs were much thinner, obviously weaker than her body, and she was struggling to get out. She must be disabled, he thought.

"I am Immie, and I have been waiting for you. Walk with me," she said.

Mikael did not question why this young child was sitting alone in an expensive electric car or why she asked him to walk with her. This seemed normal to him.

She grabbed his hand, and they walked down the trail toward the forest together. "Close your eyes." Immie ordered, "and now open them." Suddenly, they were standing by healing springs with large boulders in them.

"Did you just teleport us?" Mikael asked but was not surprised or shocked.

"Sit on that boulder," she pointed to a flat boulder that stood out like a throne overseeing the spring. Immie climbed onto the smaller one next to his.

"These stones are warm. This is a hot spring!" Mikael marveled.

Immie just smiled, closed her eyes, and sat in quiet meditation. Mikael felt awkward but followed. He closed his eyes and unexpectedly felt something move in his chest.

Did my heart just flutter, he wondered.

Something surprising happened as his heart opened to all sorts of emotions. Time stood still, and no one knew how much of it had passed. Mikael's thoughts slipped away from his ordinary life, and his mind was filled with totally different thoughts, thoughts of unconditional love for humanity. The love he felt in his heart spread throughout his whole body. It was an incredible feeling that was new to him. He felt love for all people on Earth and beyond into infinity and how much he is loved in return. Mikael's consciousness expanded, and he was one with everyone and everything there was. If he could stay here, sitting on the warm rock, he would choose to stay forever. He realized that this was not a normal human feeling and that he was not an ordinary human being; much more of him opened up at that moment.

"Let's cut to the chase. You know I am an alien," the words coming from Immie broke his thoughts.

Shock struck Mikael's body like lightning. The euphoria from being in love turned into a churning fear in his stomach, making him feel slightly nauseated. Almost in a whisper, he asked, "Did you come from the same group as me?" Mikael was unsure if he should feel afraid or relieved that they found him. He looked into Immie's eyes and saw a very old soul. Can I trust her? She smiled and opened her hand, and in the center of her palm rested a green stone that looked like a bumpy piece of green glass with a texture that reminded him of rough reptilian skin.

In bed in his small but masculinely elegant condo, Mikael woke up disoriented. He tried shutting his eyes tight to go back to sleep. For the first time in his life, he did not care if he missed a day of work; he needed to know more. Mikael's thoughts raced through his bewildered head. What was that place? Who is Immie? Am I an alien? God dammit, Am I an alien? And what was that stone? Why did she show it to me? Why did I have to wake up before I knew all the answers? Minute by minute, he was increasingly annoyed until he worked himself into an agitated state and got out of bed. He walked into the bathroom, looked into the mirror, and began talking to himself, "Mikael, you have officially gone crazy. It was just a dream, nothing else, just a play of the imagination. A cold shower should fix you right up."

When the cold water hit his skin, he was not feeling any better, so he promised himself a good, strong cup of coffee, a decent breakfast, and long hours at work to get his senses back in order.

Back in his Manhattan office, the phone kept ringing. Clients felt anxious and edgy, matching his mood. All the electronics had an extra high-pitched sound, piercing his ears and giving him a headache.

What the heck is happening to me? Do they always sound like that, he wondered.

While he sat in on a corporate meeting, he felt, for the first time, the energy of others and could read their minds just like reading the morning newspaper. The news hit a new low - greed, showing off ego, dominance, and jealousy. He started to feel as if the whole room was spinning, and this made him feel nauseated, like in his dream the night before.

"Are you okay, Mikael?" asked his boss. "Yeah, I think I am just coming down with a cold, sorry," he lied. He did not understand what was happening to him.

"Well, just pop some magic pills tonight and be here nice and early tomorrow. We do not have time for a cold," grumbled his boss.

"Yes, sir," he answered.

Mikael worked hard to get where he was. He sacrificed all his happiness to be successful among the big guys, guys that mattered. At least, that is what he used to think. Before his dream last night, all that was important to him was money and status, which meant safety, security, and well-deserved success. He did not come from a good, supportive family, nor did he have friends and acquaintances who'd recommended him for a good job. It was just him and his blood and sweat. He thought of himself as honest, decent, and hardworking, unlike some brown-nosed people he worked with. It took a while, but he earned respect for his qualities, and clients trusted him. His colleagues teased him a lot, and they could never understand why particular clients with high portfolios specifically requested his assistance. He knew why; it was because his work had integrity, and he was always honest and upfront, even about the risks they might be taking. He made it in the world of the big guys and was sure his next promotion was his. Then, I can finally have a little bit more time for fun and life, he would tell himself.

A lovely woman clad in a stylish yet comfortable dress with dark, sandy blond hair and a healthy tan walked into his office around 6 p.m. Her presence felt like magic. "There's my big brother, working as if there is no tomorrow," she said with a big, cheerful smile as she walked behind his desk and kissed his cheek. How are you? And why are you looking ...so pale and tired?"

"I was just fine until you came in," he said, a little annoyed, "What can I do for you, Katy?"

"How about dinner with your favorite sister?" she smiled.

"You are my only sister." When he looked at her, he thought she must have been a witch in the past, and people just fell under her spell. "Don't do that witch charm on me," he laughed and added regretfully, "I am sorry, I can't. I still have some work to do."

"You always have work to do," she said, "And this is why I brought dinner to you. If that's the only way to enjoy my time with you, I'll take it." She lifted the paper bag she held in her hand, "Time to feast."

"You know I love you, Katy. I guess I can spare a few minutes. I am starving. Thank you."

"Oh, don't get sappy with me. Usually, you are snappy and not sappy. Something is wrong; I can sense it. Put those papers away. Do you want to tell me about it?" She took out two bento boxes of Japanese food from the paper bag. You can have my leftovers," she teased.

"Ugh," he sighed.

"Why ugh? You've eaten my leftovers for as long as I can remember. Just because we are in your sophisticated office doesn't mean it has to be different. I won't tell anyone, I promise," she laughed softly. They didn't have a good family growing up, but they always had each other; they had bonds beyond this lifetime, and she was sure of that.

"I have something else for you," she reached into her purse and took out a small box with her business logo engraved on the top. Katy rubbed her thumb gently over it and felt such gratitude. It was Mikael who encouraged her to open her shop; he invested his money in her and taught her to be a successful businesswoman. If it had been up to her, she would just run it on her emotions, love, and kindness and be penniless, maybe even homeless, as she knew nothing about business. Men have a brain for this kind of thing. He often told her, "And you have the heart and ancient skills that are the center of your eccentric little shop." She reminisced silently. Katy had named her shop "Crystal Cures and Herbal Remedies."

She handed him the box. "There you go. Open it!" she urged him. "I had a new shipment today, and once I held this one in my hand, I knew in my heart that it was meant for you. I know you aren't crazy about all this, but you must accept this one, Mikael."

"Like I had to accept the protection charm for my car, the crystal essence to keep my brain sharp, and the faceted crystal for the window to bring rainbow into my life?" he was about to continue. "Shush and open it," she interjected with a full mouth and gestured with her chopsticks.

"Yes, ma'am."

He took the small box, lifted the lid, and looked at the contents inside. There it was again! Something in his chest rolled up and down, but he was sure it was not his heart jumping this time. He leaned back in his chair and stared in disbelief.

"Do you like it?" She could see he was surprised, and it pleased her. It was a rare moment, and it took a lot to knock his breath out.

"How is this possible?" he said in disbelief, primarily to himself. In the box was the green stone from his dream, the one Immie held in her hand just before he woke up.

"I placed my order, and this baby came from the Czech Republic. Once I touched it, I felt there was a message inside," she intentionally paused. "Bring me to Mikael," she said in a deep, slow, dramatic voice for the right spooky effect, "And bring Japanese food, too," she added jokingly. "But seriously, you know how I sense those things that you don't always believe in, but I felt you must have this stone. It's lovely, isn't it?"

Gently, Mikael picked it up from the box and cradled it in his palm, and a warm feeling began to spread through his body. In his mind he was back in his dream.

Immie held the stone for him to see. "This is Moldavite. Hold it while I speak. About fifteen million years ago, a meteorite from Pleiades fell to the Earth. Its impact created an incredible force that combined

Cosmic energy and Earth energy, forming stones like this one," she paused.

"Earth," she gestured with her hand all around, "Is a place of duality. Everything here has at least two purposes. It's a natural law. The Cosmic meteorite created destruction, and at that same moment, the Earth created healing for the destruction. See, duality has harmony; to every action, there is a reaction. Healing, in this case, will be physical and emotional healing. With the rebirth and the re-growth of the Plant and Animal Kingdom, they were most affected."

"What about humans?" he blurted out.

She smiled compassionately, "Humans are animals, and fifteen million years ago, this animal looked very different than it does today." Then she became serious: "Fifteen million years ago, no one would entertain the possibility that one day, our extraterrestrial souls would be living within an animal vessel on Earth."

"Immie, am I an alien?"

"You are one of those extraterrestrial souls living in the human body. You have been on Earth since Atlantis and have been helping our kind and humanity since then."

"This place, this land of 33 acres including these hot springs, you will buy in the future," stated Immie

"It's impossible," Mikael started to speak as she interrupted him.

"Mikael, we do not have too much time. Listen to me. I will find a way to get this stone to you in real life.

You must have it. Remember, there is no such thing as a coincidence. I will visit you a few more times to teach you."

"Immie, how do I find this place? Tell me what it's called. Give me a hint," he pleaded desperately.

"I cannot do that. You have to find it on your own."

"But how?"

"Follow your alien compass," was the last thing he heard.

"Mikael! Mikael!" his sister's loud voice brought him back, "You zoned out for a few seconds."

"A few seconds? It felt much longer than a few seconds," he mumbled as he pushed his food away.

"Now you are freaking me out," she said, eyeing him carefully. "What is happening to my brother? He has always thought of the crystals I gave him as trinkets and nothing more, and he tolerated them because he loves me," thought Katy. It was true; she felt this Moldavite was for him, but so was the car protection charm she made him several years ago. However, she could see that he made a conscious connection this time.

Mikael stood up and started packing up the leftover food. "Come on, we are done here. Let's go to my place, and I'll tell you about my dream. You'll probably understand it better than I, and maybe after that, I can get back to my normal life."

CHAPTER 8

MINTAKA

PAY IT FORWARD
Maggie's Life

"Maggie, look at these coffee bags! They just arrived. OMG, OMG, my art is on your coffee bags!" Frankie shouted with delight. "I am going to do the happy dance, and you should join me!"

Maggie smiled at her friend from behind the counter, "I don't know, Frankie, I don't know," she said sarcastically, pretending to be worried. George raised his eyebrows as he looked at Maggie.

"You hate it, just say it. You hate it. I can't take it," demanded Frankie as she suddenly started to feel worried.

"Would you two stop teasing each other," George interjected, "Frankie, it's amazing. People will want to frame their coffee bags and pass them down from generation to generation as an heirloom piece."

"Seriously?" Frankie ran to him and gave him a big hug.

"Seriously," Maggie chimed in and walked toward them. "Sit down, Frankie. I have to tell you something."

"Hope it's good," smiled Frankie.

"It's better than that. I want you to create your own business," Maggie said seriously.

"Are you firing me? Look, if you hate the picture, you can just tell me. We have been friends since school, Maggie," Frankie was about to cry.

"Stop that silly, I am not sick in the head. How could I fire my best employee? I would get uninvited from all of your holiday dinners. And look at George. He is looking forward to Thanksgiving dinner as much as I am. I want to give you an opportunity to grow something you like. George gave it to me by giving me start-up money. And I want to pay it forward," she turned to George and squeezed his hand, "Thank you again," she whispered.

"No need to thank me anymore, sweetheart," said George, smiling.

By now, George was spending much of his time in the coolest coffee shop in the neighborhood. Maggie's Beings was becoming popular day by day.

"Maggie's Beings," George mused with a thoughtful look on his face.

As if more than spending all of his time here was needed, he also volunteered to fix little things here and there. George did not need money; he had found family, which was priceless. He thought of Maggie and Frankie as grown-up children, whom he and his wife had never had. Mary would have loved them, too, he thought tenderly.

"I've thought about this for a while, and I have been feeling guidance telling me that selling my signature blend beans will be a hit and that we will eventually franchise," Maggie said while tapping her hand on her chest.

"Frankie, I want you to create a merchandise line with shirts, mugs, tumblers, fridge magnets, etc., all with my logo and your artwork on them."

Frankie just sat there and stared.

"You are an incredible artist, and I am blessed to have you as a friend," she said, swallowing her emotions before she cried. "Just think about it, Frankie. You can make prints of your artwork so people can hang them on their walls instead of pressing coffee bags."

"I want you to be my business partner in merchandise," she chirped. "We will start with tiny orders and grow it from there. It will be another source of advertisement and a new source of income. I'll offer you 50% of that income, which will be your baby. All you have to do is invest your talent, run this part of the business, and believe in us."

"Frankie?" both George and Maggie said at the same time.

"This is the best day of my life," Frankie said before she broke into waterfalls of happiness.

DEAD END STREET
Mikael's Life

Mikael was driving home from work. It was late, and it was getting dark. Traffic was painful, and he felt that he shouldn't have driven, though driving was an impulse he had that morning. Now, he began to think he should have taken the subway as usual.

A few months had passed, and he couldn't get the dream out of his head. Katy had wrapped the Moldavite she had given him in gold wire so he could wear it on a necklace, keeping it close to his heart. But since that day, he has had no dreams or encounters with Immie.

"Maybe it was just a dream, and I am being obsessive," he told himself, trying to focus on the road.

At first, he was in denial regarding his ego and then angry. What made matters worse was that he did not know how to change his life, let alone where to begin. He knew that something happened to him that day, something that changed him forever. He started reading the spiritual books his sister recommended, particularly ones addressing the ego. Until he received the stone, his job was everything to him. He was happy with his life. Now, he was dealing with anxiety and low-grade depression, and he wanted his old self back.

Mikael thought about the last time he talked to Katy. She smiled and said, "It will all come together at the right time." He was impatient.

While his life in review was like a movie playing before him, Mikael noted that the need for financial safety was his biggest drive from childhood. Many times, he and Katy were scared, hungry, and routinely changing schools because they kept moving. Stability and safety are what he wanted for the two of them, even if his dream job makes him feel empty now.

How can I go and do something else? What else can I do if I don't know how to do anything else? Mikael's thoughts left him feeling defeated. He graduated with a business degree, was at the top of his class, and became a financial adviser. He did not like all the people he worked with, especially now when, as Katy explained, he could empathically sense their true selves, and gosh, he could read their minds, which should have been more shocking than he thought. He knew that his supervisor was secretly cheating on his wife, yet his wife brought him a homemade lunch every single day at the same time, and for thirty precious minutes, they seemed like lovebirds. If she only knew, he shivered, pushing those thoughts away.

Traffic was a killer. Suddenly, he started to feel dizzy, and his vision blurred slightly. This dizziness set off a shortness of breath and chest pains, which alarmed him. Mikael thought he was having a heart attack. He was stuck in traffic, and his phone was in the car trunk in his bag.

What am I going to do? He was trying to think.

A few feet ahead of him was a sign for a dead-end street. He was trying to calm himself down to safely turn to this street and maybe get to his phone. Panic was creeping in. This is ironic. I'm going to die on a dead-end street; this is how my life feels, like a dead end. His chest hurt, his breath was labored, and he thought he was about to pass out.

"At least I won't cause a traffic jam," he muttered

With great effort, he turned and parked on the side of the dead-end street.

"Mikael!"

He looked to his right to find where the voice was coming from.

"Immie?" he tried to focus his eyes, "Am I dying?"

She put her hand on his chest, and he could feel warm energy soothing him. "Calm down, Mikael. Take slow, deep breaths. You are having a panic attack."

"I'm not dying?" he asked.

"No," she said calmly, smiling a little.

"Immie, I didn't find that place yet."

"You worry too much, Mikael; it will come at the right time."

Now, she sounds like my sister. He thought, annoyed.

"How is it possible you are here. Am I dreaming?"

"You are not dreaming. Just keep breathing. See, it's going away; drink your water," she pointed to his half-full water bottle. You need to take better care of yourself, Mikael." It looked ironic that a six-year-old was scolding him and, at the same time, saving him from a panic attack. "I'm bi-located here to tell you a story," she shifted in her seat.

"You and I had a life together in Mintaka."

"Mintaka?" he raised his eyebrow.

"Just listen now. We have only a certain amount of time," Immie stated.

"You have had many incarnations in this Universe, and the last incarnation before Earth was in the Orion constellation, on Mintaka. Our people are amphibious beings. Think of your childhood in this life, Mikael; you were always fascinated with frogs because they reminded you of a place where your soul felt at home, not by their looks but by their abilities. You are a good swimmer, and you equally love water as much as you love nature and your life in the city."

Mikael thought of the summer when he was about 6 years old when he was trying to convince his friends he could breathe underwater. They made fun of him and called him a freak.

"Let me show you your home," Immie said, touching his forehead with the tip of her finger.

Mikael saw a spark of light, and it seemed like he was traveling through a tunnel faster than the speed of light. Then he saw thriving nature, lush green grass, trees, tall plants, and exotic flowers. He could even smell the scent of the water. He tried to find a description in his mind for this place, something like a subtropical climate with lots of lagoons, marshes, and water. It was pristine and breathtaking. Then he saw a natural pool of emerald green water, the color of his eyes. He remembered how he used to dive in and sit at the bottom for a long time, telepathically communicating with his friends. He remembered them. This was home.

"Hot springs, they have hot springs here," he thought excitedly.

"These hot springs have rare healing properties and have been the best-kept secret of our society for generations," said Immie.

Mikael was directed towards a few tall houses, smartly positioned amongst the green plants and trees. They looked like Japanese Pagodas, yet he knew they were not used as shrines. They were houses meant for living. They were not separated into condos as tall buildings on Earth would be. In these pagodas, life meant union, fairness, caring, sharing, kindness, and love amongst everyone who lived there. And it felt like a lot of beings could live in one pagoda.

"Mik'El?" a woman called his name. It sounded a little different, yet he knew it was his name. He turned and faced an older woman, and his heart almost stopped.

"Mom?" he asked slowly.

She nodded, and her eyes, emerald green as his, were filled with tears. As he fell into a tight embrace in his mother's arms, he broke into sobs.

"SShhh, Mik'El, it's okay. You have to control your emotions," whispered Immie in his ear. Otherwise, you'll lose the connection."

He could hear Immie and knew she was sitting in the car with him. He could also feel his mother and knew he was on Mintaka. He took a deep breath and calmed down. He needed to know more.

His mother gestured for him to sit down beside her. "Life used to be simple here, and we liked it that way," she paused, "For thousands of years, we lived happily and felt safe here. Even though we were positioned in the territory of the Dark Lords, they left us alone as we appeared to have no useful military skills; therefore, we were not useful to them."

"One day, a spaceship crashed onto our planet carrying Dark Lords from Rigel. They all died except for one. His vital signs were weak, and he was hardly alive; his body was gruesomely damaged. Our people pulled him out, and since we are naturally caring, we did not judge where he came from. They carried him to the healing hot spring and, over time, nursed him back to full, vigorous health. At first, we held back our friendship, but it was hard not to like him. He had charisma, and he was grateful for our care. He became our friend, and we trusted him. We began to show him more of our life, which we have carefully safeguarded. He became fascinated with the power of our healing waters, the children playing underwater for prolonged periods, and our mental abilities, especially telepathy, mind reading, and remote viewing."

Mikael's interest peaked when his mother mentioned the mental abilities of his people.

"There came a time when life on our planet was not good enough for him, as he had ambitions we did not want to understand. He found a way to contact his people and left. We would not hold him as a prisoner, and we let him go."

"In a matter of time, he came back with others. We felt betrayed. They demanded to know the secrets of our healing water. They asked us how it was possible to bring the almost-dead back to life? They harmed their own people and threw them into the spring to satisfy their curiosity, and when they saw that they could heal, they claimed the hot springs as their property. They believed that the natural phenomena of Mintaka created the healing water. We let them believe that."

"We protected the knowledge of the healing springs. Mik'El, we are the guardians of the healing water. We also guard the secret of how these hot springs truly work. Only our wise elders know, and the knowledge is passed down through generations."

"Over time, as they took over our planet, the healing water slowly lost its full effect. They were angry, and they began to resent us, to control us." She became quiet for a little while. It looked like she was collecting her emotions for what she would say next.

"They took away our children to become their spies, their prisoners," she said, trying to hold back her tears.

She could feel his anger rise, and she gently touched his hand. "Mik'El, do not feel anger. Learn to forgive them. So much has changed since then. It is our past, and it shaped you into who you are, but now it is up to you to choose who you want to be. This does not exist anymore," she motioned to the scene before him.

"What you are seeing now is my memory saved for you. You may have seen it in your previous lives; it is like a time capsule of memories, but in each incarnation, your mind creates a kind of amnesia to block your recollection of this memory. I want you to know that I am long gone and at peace, but I know you will remember one day. You will remember in your soul and search for the truth," she paused.

"They took you when you were still a child, a long time ago. They took all of our children and programmed them to serve the system of the Dark Lords. We heard you were put into the camps and were trained to be a psychic spy soldier. Mintakans have a strong nervous system and incredible mind capacity. Your amphibious abilities have fine-tuned your mind, giving you the ability to communicate underwater and on the land."

"They managed to block your memories of home so you would forget you have a kind and caring soul. Any being who remembers unconditional love cannot carry out acts of cruelty that come naturally to the Dark Lords. They are the masters of Intelligent Mind programs and mind control. In their camps, you were trained to control your thoughts and eliminate your emotions. You were taught that emotions and love are weaknesses. Weakness was punished gruesomely on Rigel."

She patted his cheek gently, "You have a powerful and beautiful mind, Mik'El, and you have been taken away against your will from home, from me. With their programming, you had to cope with that new life and forget who you were. You became a really good psychic spy, and they won a lot of wars because of beings like you. Eventually, you were convinced that they were doing the right thing.

"This can't be," said Mikael in disbelief. Did I become a Dark Lord? Did I intentionally harm others?

"Yes," she was reading his mind, "This is true, and you need to forgive yourself and understand why this happened to you. In essence, you never become one of them. You have always been mind-controlled by them, ruled by fears; you never had the freedom of your soul to choose who you wanted to be. To survive and protect those you cared about, you had to become who they wanted you to be. If you chose not to follow their orders, others would die. You were just a child when you had to decide the fate of those you knew."

Mikael started to remember, "In the camps, they told us that if we did not pledge our souls to them, if we didn't master the skills that the Dark Lords wanted us to perform, they would kill our families on Mintaka. I can still hear children crying. I know they killed some of them to show that they were serious. I had to become strong for them. I believed that if I accepted this change, they would follow me, and I could save them. They did, and I swore to myself that one day, I would help them remember who they truly are and help them heal the nasty scars the Dark Lords gave us. I am sorry, mother, I disappointed you. I felt I had no choice." Mikael felt sharp pains in his stomach and regret.

Suddenly, his workplace flashed in his mind. I could never be like them. They work me like a horse, but others get the promotions. Somehow, they know that I am not like them. I'm always controlled by someone else. It is so clear now, Mikael thought.

"You did not disappoint me, Mik'El. You did save them. You helped them ease their suffering with acceptance. I know who you are inside; I know you. Your intentions were honorable. I love you and always will. You helped them survive. You need to forgive yourself. You need to find a way to accept yourself, to forgive yourself, and to love yourself. Other beings depend on that as well."

"I will try. But am I worthy of loving myself when I harmed others?" he said under his breath.

"Quickly now, Mik'El. You will remember these mind-controlling programs alongside your memories of home. Do not be afraid of them. Explore them. In the darkness lies hidden truths, and you will find answers to how to help others like yourself and those under mind control. Remember, Orion is not what it used to be anymore. Whatever you remember, whatever you have done, always remember me as I am the essence of you. Your soul is good, filled with unconditional love, and your mind is not dark or evil. Only those who use it to control others create endless suffering throughout this Universe. The mind is brilliant and beautiful in the hands of the soul. And Mik'El, everyone is worthy of love, even the Dark Lords."

"On Mintaka, you had equal energies, a balance of the soul and mind, or as you call it, Light and Dark. Our soul is reflected in the bountiful nature of Mintaka, which nourishes the body's emotions. Our planet was like a collective garden of our souls. It was breathtaking. Our mind was reflected in physical creations that made life easy, simple, and enjoyable for the body, like the healing springs and pagodas you have seen. On Mintaka, your soul and mind were connected in a twin flame union; on Rigal, the mind was the only flame."

"You are much more than you give yourself credit for. You are smart and caring; always remember that. I love you, my son. I am proud of the man you have become. Now I have to say fare well. May your life be a reflection of who you truly are."

"Mom! Mom! Don't leave yet!" Mikael was shouting.

Suddenly, he heard someone knocking on his car window, "Sir, are you all right?"

A little disoriented, he looked around. Immie was gone, but he was still sitting in his car. It was dark outside, and he was probably shouting out loud. His face was wet from tears; he was a mess.

Mikael cleared his throat as he rolled down the window a bit, "I'm fine. I wasn't feeling too good, so I pulled over to rest a little. I guess I fell asleep. I am about to go now. I'm sorry if I alarmed you."

"All right. Drive safe," said the older gentleman.

Mikael started his car and left.

CHAPTER 9

MIND CONTROL

HAUNTING FEARS
Mikael's Life

Since the evening Mikael spoke with his mother in Mintaka, he has felt attacked by what he thought could only be negative energy. He was hearing high-pitched noises again. He couldn't hear it with his physical ears, but inside his head, it felt like someone was scratching nails on a chalkboard. It was unbearable. His head was pounding, and it felt inside as if a small brain was at war with a large brain, battling for control.

"Not everything is a psychic attack," said Katy patiently. They were cramped in her small office in the back of her shop.

"Katy," he said, annoyed. "You know I'm not the kind of person who gets scared easily, yet this," he waved his hand above his head, "This scares the hell out of me. What if I'm having a mental breakdown? I'm having these thoughts that I'm a horrible person, and that I'm a failure, these mistakes from my past are haunting me. This is not me. What if, in that life, I became just as evil as they were?"

"Are you afraid of them?" she asked directly.

"Of who?"

"The Dark Lords who took you away from Mintaka. Are you afraid they will find you again?

"Come on, it doesn't make any sense," said Mikael

"Yes or no, Mikael."

"Maybe," he said reluctantly.

She took a deep breath and began to scan his energy. "You feel darkness shadowing you. You feel the presence of someone or something. Like it can touch you at any time, and if it does, if it succeeds, you will die. You can't sleep because you no longer feel safe in the dark of night," she paused, tapping her fingers on her face, reading his energy and thinking, "And your emotions fluctuate between shame and guilt and fear that someone will find out who you are and what you have done, even though you don't really know what that may be. It doesn't make sense to you, and it scares the hell out of you."

His eyes were laser-focused on her, and he felt mildly embarrassed. "Yes," he added quietly, "Katy, no one can know. I would lose my reputation," he swallowed hard and rubbed his hands over his face. He was visibly tired.

"Can't you just remove it? You do energy work for others. I have seen you. I didn't always believe in that. I'm sorry, but I do now."

"I wish I could, but this is out of my reach. You are different from most, and you are not hopeless. You are starting to remember your life beyond Earth—a life when you were an alien. Mikael, you are also remembering you had extraordinary abilities. There must be a reason for all of this, and this is your journey to find yourself. I can only guide you," Katy was trying to encourage him.

"What should I do?" his voice was desperate.

"You need to connect with the boy you were in Mintaka, the boy who was taken away from his family against his will. You need to remember him before and after his abduction. You have to help him understand what happened, forgive those who have done this to him, and, most importantly, help him forgive himself. This is the way to remember more of who you are," she said compassionately.

"Right now, you are acting like a scared little boy. Do you really think you would feel more in control when angry, seeking vengeance, or denying that anything like this happened?

Mikael just sat there, looking frustrated.

Anger is not the answer, Mikael, and it will not go away until YOU deal with it."

"Mik'El was just a child. The first part of his life was beautiful, filled with love and happiness. Feel what it was like to be him as he was then when he had aspirations and dreams about the future," she put her hand on his heart and looked into his eyes. "What you remember is only a fraction of the truth. You are now living in the emotions of what happened when he was taken away to Rigel. Anger, fear, and hopelessness. Do not be afraid to become him and experience him as one with who you are now," she paused, weighing her words.

"They took you because you had amazing psychic abilities. That was the one and only reason they wanted you. And it seems to me that your abilities and memories of who you were are returning."

Mikael nodded in agreement.

"You need to heal your soul before gaining them all back. What would you do with them if you didn't first heal these ancient fears and anger? Would you really use them for the good of everyone or for what YOU think would be good?"

Mikael was taking in every word she said as he got up and paced the small office.

Katy continued, "Think about it. How many times, as Mik'El, you must have hated who you were and what you could do. How many times did you wish you were "normal" because you thought being different caused pain to everyone you loved and cared about? You cannot renounce who you are. It's more complicated than cutting your hand off. This is part of you. It always has been and always will be. You have the same problem in this life. It's time to accept yourself, Mikael."

Mikael sat down in defeat.

"You were a child, Mikael, and you were torn between impossible decisions. You had to either use your abilities and cause harm to others, strangers you did not know, or not use them and bring harm to those you loved? Those are hard decisions to make."

"The darkness you feel is not coming from those that took you from your home. You are projecting your dark monster that protects you from reaching your abilities. Something inside of you makes you believe that you are so bad that the monster is coming for you."

"And there is something else, something that is orchestrating all of this so you can find the truth, Mikael. You will never find it if you are afraid of what you may discover. I think that that "something" is your soul."

"You have awakened into your own shadow, your pain, your shame, your regrets. I wish I could remove that from you, but I don't have that ability. Even if I could, it would not be right. I would just wipe your memory. I would be just like them. Your soul screams in pain so your ego can find the truth that connects it to the brilliant alien mind that you have."

"How do you know all this?" questioned Mikael.

"I feel it inside of me. I feel like someone is talking to you through me," she answered honestly, giving him a long, compassionate look. "Go home, meditate, and walk into your own cave of darkness, your heart. Observe this darkness instead of blaming others for it.

And for the sake of this conversation, you were brainwashed to become one of them."

"Not by my choice, remember? Not by my free will," he said, exhausted.

"What did your mother tell you, hmm?" she paused. His business mind was brilliant, but sometimes he needed more common sense.

"She told you to 'forgive yourself and forgive them,' she also told you that 'Orion is not what it used to be,' and that means the Dark Lords are either long gone by now, or they have transformed into good guys."

He looked at her, considering what she had just said, "How can you be sure?"

"Mikael, look at me. Look into my eyes," she said strictly, looking at him, "Have I ever lied to you?"

"No."

"I know you are afraid of what you might discover about yourself, but to me, you are Mikael, my big brother. You act all tough, but you have a good heart, and I will love you no matter what," she smiled.

"If any of those Dark Lords wanted to destroy you, they would have done so by now. After all, you are just mortal, so why be afraid of them?"

"You have a point," he answered slowly.

"If they wanted to enslave you again, they would just load you into a spaceship and carry you into the depths of the Universe. Wouldn't it be easy for them to do so?" she held herself from laughing.

"Yes," he seemed to consider this way too seriously.

122

"If they wanted to brainwash you again into doing their bidding like a puppet, would you be listening to me now?

"Okay, I see your point," he snapped a little.

"Now, stop being ridiculous, meditate, and connect with that darkness. Think about it, Mikael. What is the worst thing that can happen to you?" she asked compassionately.

"I will die, and there will be no one to take care of you," he said sincerely.

She felt really sorry for him. "See, we are getting somewhere. You need to conquer your inner fears and transform them into healthy courage," she said.

"Also, let's remember that I have a thriving business, and I've been taking care of myself pretty well; plus, I have a date tonight. So, If you die tonight, I will be heartbroken. But Mikael, I will make it, and I will meet you again," she said in a playful manner.

THE SPIDER IMPLANT
Mikael's Life

Later that evening, Mikael sat in silent meditation. Intentionally, he focused on his heart chakra and walked into his cave of darkness. It took considerable time, but he accepted Mik'El's and others' fate from his Mintaka home. He forgave the Dark Lords and himself.

He even felt rays of unselfish love. Exhausted, he fell into a deep sleep.

Mikael woke up in the middle of the night, startled from his sleep. The scratching noise he had been hearing was back, and he felt it was about time he followed this lead. Holding neutral energy as Katy had taught him, he promised himself he would not judge whatever he saw. Heart–mind connection, he thought.

He was doing well. In his mind, he followed this noisy, annoying energy above his physical body, a little bit to the right. Then he saw it, perched on the outer edge of what he felt was his astral field. It startled him initially, but then he reminded himself that he would not judge what he saw and would stay neutral to any discovery. He saw a black shape that looked like a spider. It was large, with long, slender legs. It was almost like an Earth spider but more mechanical-looking.

It shocked him at first, but Mikael held his focus and neutral energy and just observed it. The spider was not really moving. It was just staying in its place. Mikael felt like it had been there for a while like it was at home and very comfortable.

He could not sense its motives for being there, but his thoughts began streaming in.

Is this from Rigel? Does it control me? Does it feed off of my negative thoughts? Does it want to block my progress in life? He intuitively knew it was extraterrestrial in nature.

Suddenly, he saw through Mik'El's eyes. He was much older than the boy he had seen before and was at some kind of school.

Mik'El was standing before a man he called Master. He was holding the same spider in his hand, showing the students.

"This is an implant, the most advanced in AI technology. It is programmed to attach to the mind frequency through your nervous system, your electric circuit. The frequency of this implant can be tuned for various effects. Telepathy is one of them, and mind synchronization with AI is another. When everyone is implanted with this device, we will control their mind programs as a collective," stated the Master.

"Do you mean we will be able to control everyone's minds?" Mik'El asked.

"Of course. We want ultimate power. We cannot rely solely on your kind to read minds and project the controlling thoughts we need to be transmitted."

"You do not trust me?" asked Mik'El.

"Trust no one, Mik'El, you will survive longer," the Master told him in a strict voice.

"This," said the Master, as he eyed the spider, "can read your mind. It can also control your mind by suggesting that the thoughts you are given are your own. It is the most sophisticated technology in the science of the mind. If we program this device with negative thoughts, it will also produce negative thoughts on a grander scale. The spider will search your recorded memories and find your biggest weakness. Then, it will create corresponding actions and reactions throughout your electrical currents. As you already know, the mind has an electrical circuit. This technology will eventually replace psychic mind spies, as there is a shortage of your kind."

"But you, Mik'El, you are different. You have always been the smartest one," remarked the Master.

You are a rare gem and one of very few who has made it this far, though the Master, recalling the electric shocks that they were using to program him for their agenda. He was their best subject to date.

"Will this also suppress emotions? Will they be like us, not feeling emotions?" asked Mik'El.

"That is what we want, yes. Imagine every being in this Universe synchronized to only one program, our program," he felt a greedy power surging through him.

Mik'El felt a physical pain in his heart. The Master looked at him suspiciously and spoke louder to intimidate him. They worked too hard to suppress his emotions. He was not going to lose him.

"Why would you want to feel longing emotions when you follow the Path of the Mind? We are the most intelligent beings. We have the most advanced technology. We have safety, ambition, authority, force, and control and rely on ourselves. We do not need anything else," the Master said in an authoritarian tone.

"What about love?" Mik'El blurted out without considering the consequences.

"Love!" the Master screamed. "Love is weakness. Emotional feelings are a weakness that can control us, and that is WHY we control them. I never want to hear THAT word from you again. Do you understand?"

Mik'El nodded his head quickly.

In a much calmer voice, the Master continued, "The spider controls only your thoughts, as it is attached to the mind frequency. You, as a being with a soul, create emotions based on your thoughts. There are some Universal laws we cannot override," he paused thinking. "At least for now," he sneered.

"Unfortunately, we need the soul to animate this body, but we can shut it up by controlling the thoughts. Our AI technology will do that and more for us. If you want to feel lust or satisfaction, you can. You can turn its frequency up or down with just a click of a button." Then, with an unsavory grin, he added, "The Maidens of the Pleiades will please our bodies, and we will decide how they spend their time. Mik'El, can you see this vision? Imagine our control over ALL star nations."

"Yes, Master," he answered. Mik'El felt the electric vibrations of his teacher, representing greed, wants, and needs.

A long time ago, deep, deep inside his soul, Mik'El buried a promise that one day he would remember and awaken his soul's emotions and help others heal from this control. Until then, he would become a perfect soldier on the Path of the Mind, even though this journey was dark and troubling. He could not feel; he just knew, and no one would ever know his secret; he made sure of that.

Chapter 10

Memory of Galactic Wars

The Council
Lights of the Universe Transmission

The story of what happened in this Universe during the Galactic Wars is long and complex. It is heartbreaking to remember how many beings have been harmed, taken away from their homes, re-educated, and enslaved. How many planets have been destroyed before those on the Path of Dark and those on the Path of Light realized that we were collectively heading toward universal destruction. The story of Mik'El is a good example we would like to share with you, as we believe many of you will relate to it. We hope you find synchronicity in your life that will ultimately lead to the healing of this ancient trauma encoded in your DNA.

In the days of the Galactic Wars, we were sharing this Universe, just as you now share the Earth with every being on the planet. Uniting our forces was the only answer to ensure a future for those following us. Since you are remembering this history, you are us in the future. The future depends on you. You are not much different than we were back then, living in separation, with various beliefs, the need for control, anger, hate or love, acceptance, compassion, a holistic approach to life, and visions of a peaceful and different future. Each group fiercely protects their beliefs, and the majority is unwilling to find common ground.

We were you, and you are us. If this statement is correct, you are realizing that your soul has been journeying through this Universe for eons. You are searching for your past lives and rekindling ancient abilities. But you need to realize that you are not just a soul; you are also a mind, and they are interconnected in this Universe. Your soul is remembering, and your mind is becoming more intelligent. Look at the technological evolution in the past one hundred years. Spiritual and technological evolution go hand in hand until one tries to outsmart the other, and then destruction follows. Look into your history. The patterns are there.

Since your soul is starting to remember lives beyond the Earth, your mind is also beginning to remember. Your soul remembers your natural alien abilities, and your mind is learning to connect to the 5D alien mind and operate from that frequency. It is a common fact that an alien mind is connected to the

Universal Intelligent Mind – the source of all knowledge and power.

Your soul journeys through this Universe. It collects experiences and shares knowledge and wisdom. As a perfect gentleman, the mind accompanies the soul on all adventures. The mind and soul are co-creators, and their intention is to co-create the most perfect Universe, so they are experimenting with various scenarios. We used to think the Earth was just a tiny part of the big picture. Still, to our surprise, the Earth has proven to be the most effective and safest place to practice the law of "cause and effects" within this Universe and serves as a training ground for the soul's and the mind's symbiosis. In Lemuria, we thought we found the Earth. In Atlantis, we thought we ruled the Earth. After the cataclysm, we all, the Light and the Dark, realized our arrogance. We did not find the Earth; the Earth found us, attracted us, that she may teach us a valuable lesson – teamwork. Were we ready to learn that lesson?

The alien becomes human, and the human becomes alien again. What did we learn over those thousands of years?

The Council of the Light and Dark combined their work and efforts towards the end of the Galactic Wars. Before then, they each operated separately in different locations. During the Councils of Light and Dark conjoining, their new home base became Sirius A. This was just a new beginning on the long journey towards healing, rebuilding, learning how to coexist and thrive together, and genuinely uniting.

Eons have passed by, and you are coming full circle. Your memories are returning, and therefore, new growth opportunities are opening. You must open your heart and allow the soul to guide you on this evolutionary journey. Now that you are becoming 5D beings in your mind while still occupying a 3D body, you are learning to work with the ego, a lower vibrational counterpart to the mind. Without a good relationship with your soul, the mind will want to seduce you with the most futuristic life you can ever imagine.

Since the original separation, it is well known that the mind wants you to give up emotions, while the soul wants you to give up the comfort of advancement. Your challenge is to find how to have both. Nothing is impossible.

MIK'EL ON SIRIUS A
Mik'El's Memory

Mik'El arrived on Sirius A in a Pleiadian spaceship. It felt like only yesterday when he learned that Mintaka had almost been destroyed and is now uninhabitable. Despite his sacrifice, he had no home to return to. And even if he did, he felt he no longer belonged there. His experiences had changed him, and he had become hardened to life as he lived through the peace treaty between the Light and the Dark.

When the Galactic Wars ended, he was generously offered a new home and a new life on Electra in the Pleiades constellation. He was shocked by their generosity. It was hard at first, as he felt an urgent need for self-punishment and believed he was not worthy of having a second chance. They were patient with him, and in time, he learned that Electra was a safe haven for refugees like him. He surrendered and accepted the help because he felt that this would be a safe place to completely heal his soul wounds and learn how to master the ability to assist others in the same manner. He knew he had a long way to go.

He was seated in front of the Council and asked to share what he thought were the essential parts of his story. His voice was strong because he had painfully learned how to control his emotions.

"At first, when I learned that the wars were finally over, I just wanted to die, and then somewhere deep in my soul, I remembered my vow to help others heal from the trauma of the wars. For a while, it was the only thing that gave me a reason to go on," said Mik'El, with distance in his voice.

"When I arrived at Rigel, I missed my mother and home. I thought that if I closed my eyes tight, I could find myself sitting at the bottom of the lagoon, hearing my mother's voice calling me for dinner. I was praying that what was happening to us was just a dream, a nightmare that would go away when I woke up. But this was our reality. When I opened my eyes, all I saw were my friends locked in the same room with me, crying in despair. We were beaten and tortured every time we refused to cooperate. I thought I would never become like those cruel Masters who were in charge of our reprogramming. And for the first time in my life, I hated someone. I hated them."

Signs of compassion spread throughout the Council.

Mik'El continued, "Then they started killing us, slowly, painfully, and we were forced to watch. Showing emotion was considered a weakness; when you cried, made a noise, or cringed, you were next. They didn't always kill you that day. They made us wait, sometimes for days."

"I looked at my brothers and sisters from Mintaka, and I made a decision. I had to make it easier for them to survive. If I changed, I knew they would follow me, and it would be easier for us to listen to these cruel beings until I could find a way to rescue us all. I vowed to myself that I would find a way, but I must admit, I never did. I regret that. I became lost in their cruel ways and forgot who I was."

ORION'S ACKNOWLEDGMENT
Orion Transmission

In the Orion constellation, we became mind-dominated beings. When our journey started, we had no intention of becoming Dark. Our original desire was intelligence, intellectuality, and its application into any possible field. For this reason, we had chosen to experience a Path of the Mind, and we eventually became seduced by its power. We became addicted to feeling important, powerful, and almost invincible. As with any addiction, you crave more.

As thousands of years passed, several incarnations were accomplished, and we fell deeper into the self-created isolation of our own minds. The need to be in control of everything turned into our obsession. We were disconnected from our soul's emotions and hypnotized by our own controlling alien mind. We cannot blame anyone for this. We can only acknowledge our own mistakes and learn from them.

The original essence of this particular Universe is the Intelligent Mind. It is the most brilliant mind you can possibly imagine. The Intelligent Mind is the most creative and destructive power in this Universe. As impressive as it sounds, it is just an energy that does not misuse itself. We became part of this energy, and we misused it.

One who forges a sword does not hold power over the decisions of the one wielding the sword.

If you honor the mind and allow the soul to join in its creative expression, the outcome is beyond what words can express, and this Universe will be perfect. If you think you can control your mind, it will temporarily give you "a power trip, " leaving you craving more. Many of us have tried, and no one ever has succeeded. The craving will numb your good intuitive senses, and you will be guided by the forces of other beings who control minds, seducing you with greed, and you will do THEIR bidding by your own free will; maybe you will become one of them. The outcome is destructive, but you will be too blind to see it.

We are sharing this wisdom with you so that you will know that no mysterious force in this Universe can cause you intentional misery. This Universe supports life, and its goal is to help it thrive. Individual, separated minds, controlled by ego – whether human or alien are the forces behind all wrongdoing on Earth and in the Universe. In other words, what we have learned is that we, collectively, are our own worst enemies. Wars, the need for power and control, are a useless waste of energy.

OFFICE OF CHOICE
Sirian Transmission

When the soul group entered this Universe, the mind and the soul created a union in the body. They both wanted to have unique experiences of their co-creation; therefore, the "Office of Choice" was created.

136

As a unique being, having both male and female qualities, you had the option to choose one or the other for your life experience - either the Path of the Soul, which is considered the Path of Light, or the Path of the Mind, also called the Path of Dark.

To describe this, imagine that you are coming to this office to plan for your next life, just like you would if you were going to a travel agency to plan your next vacation. Each constellation of star nations offers something slightly different, and you can choose your next adventure. For example, you are invited to the Pleiades to experience the Path of Light and to learn about all varieties of healing, herbs, plants, emotions, arts, and music. This is a place where the soul dominates the experience. For balance, you are also encouraged to journey to Orion, the center of the mind. You will develop your intellectual prowess, critical thinking, and decision-making. Alongside these studies, you will learn martial arts and military exercises, and you will have access to the most advanced technology and development in the Universe. This experience is dominated by the mind.

In this office, there is no good or wrong choice. It is just a decision; it is up to you to do what you will with your chosen experience.

In the beginning, it was a fun experiment. But in the end, the experience of choice led us deeper into separation from oneness and the creation of individual lives dominated by soul or mind energy. Balance was lost, and our goal is to bring this Universe back into unity consciousness.

MIND'S TENDENCY
Orion Transmission

The mind does not operate based on emotions. The mind picks the best possible scenarios for survival and executes these scenarios. The mind's energy lacks empathy to feel compassion when someone is harmed or emotionally hurt. The mind is very similar to AI. The only difference is that you can control your mind, while AI will want to control your mind completely. You do not need an AI chip to have a synchronized mind. You can keep up with AI or be more intelligent than AI, yet AI will convince someone's mind that they have control.

In truth, no one is ever in control, yet you can be the master of your destiny. AI is just a trap to stay in the same dimension for eternity.

Our life choice back then was to be dominated by mind energy. It was easier to discriminate against the soul's energy and learn how to suppress it. It is important to state that it is not natural in this Universe. No matter how evolved or simple an organism is, you must have an equal balance between mind and soul energy.

What we (Orions) are sharing now is our understanding after having had a "mind power trip" that almost destroyed this whole Universe. We want you to listen with neutral energy in your heart. The mind's wisdom energy is meant to be understood so that you are no longer subject to mind control. Through this, you avoid the same pitfalls and avoid the desire to be in control, whether those are of people, things, or places. In all of your lives in this Universe, the only thing that will stay with you forever is the knowledge and wisdom from your experiences. Everything else is of no significance.

Mik'El Continues
Mik'El's Memory

"I tried to keep in contact with my friends from Mintaka, but it was difficult. We had to follow orders to read minds, alter mind frequencies, gear them towards cooperation with the Dark Lords, and communicate telepathically, delivering secret messages or remote viewing through very long distances."

"We became their slaves, but they did not call us that. They made us feel important when they needed us and non-existent when they did not. The feeling of importance became addictive. Eventually, after many years, we had the freedom to live in our desired places, enjoy the company of others, eat the foods we liked, and even travel within the Dark sector. Never would I think of traveling to Mintaka; they made us believe that it was such a pity and shame to be born on an undeveloped planet. I completely forgot about its beauty, the love of Mintakans, and our healing springs."

Mik'El paused for a moment, processing his thoughts.

"Over time, we aspired to be like the Dark Lords. Their houses were luxurious. Many of them were rich, and they could do anything they wanted. I came to believe they were privileged because they were born on Rigel or in lavish sectors ruled by the Dark Lords. In comparison, we came from smelly swamps. The shame of our birth was programmed in our minds with a comforting suggestion that if we work hard, one day we could be like them. It was their way to hold superior order over us so they could use us, and we obediently complied. Today, I know that they would never accept us as equals, but I wanted to believe differently back then."

"Hundreds of years later, I hated Mintaka. I felt that being born there ruined my future success. If I had been born in Rigel, I would have had better opportunities and would have been accepted. I tried to make the best out of my confused life. I was angry and unhappy, and my luck seemed to be wearing thin. The innocent boy from Mintaka was gone. An angry, narcissistic man was there instead. I did everything they asked of me. I followed all the rules, yet I struggled. I was alone and hiding my poverty. If you were born on Rigel, your financial status was outstanding; for outsiders, there were severe restrictions."

With a deep breath, Mik'El continued.

"I tried my best to fake my heritage, to make people believe I was from Rigel. I lived in fear and shame that they would one day find out who I was: an amphibian from Mintaka. Those who saw our gills shrieked in disgust. My body's appearance filled me with shame. Were we that hideous? Why could I not look like them? I felt safe, covered in clothing. I learned to manipulate the minds of those around me very well, and if they believed you were like them, they liked you. They would hate and shun you if they found out you were not like them. So I lived this secret life. And because of this, I hardly had any intimate relationships, and this made me feel isolated and very lonely."

"For some reason, I felt an inner need to belong. I had made a few friends from Rigel. They gifted me things they no longer needed, and I welcomed that. I had no idea that it would only contribute to my cravings to have my needs met, and this increased my hopelessness even more. Unfortunately, their friendship was given on their unspoken terms. When they felt they needed me, I was a good friend. They never had time for me when they were with their friends and family. They did not include me. Their families often talked bad about me, shaming me, and what was worse, I knew it. I just pretended that I did not know or care. To me, they were what I wanted to become. Wealthy, powerful, influential, and I thought that when I had THAT, I would be happy."

"I was wrong."

"I realized that we were enslaved by their system, a system we all had to follow, and it became too late to realize this when some of my childhood memories started to resurface. We couldn't all be wealthy and privileged because who would then serve us? Eventually, our mind frequency was controlled by AI frequency, and our ability to act by our free will was caged. The AI frequency produced thoughts of shame, guilt, and fears of who we were, but it also produced false positive feelings of satisfaction when we did our spy work. Our life journey was controlled, and we were used for our abilities, even admired and liked when our abilities worked to perfection. Many Mintakans were discarded when their abilities diminished."

"When the Galactic Rescue Team arrived," Mik'El put both hands over his heart, turned, and gently bowed to Pleiadians to show his gratitude, "I was afraid and relieved at the same time," he continued. Our soul healing started. I knew I wished this for others, but I was not sure if I deserved this new chance of life. After all, I failed them; I failed us."

"Thank you, Mik'El, for sharing your story with us," said a member of the Sirian Council, expressions of gratitude echoed throughout the Council. "Please enjoy the hospitality of Sirius A."

After the Council retired from the meeting hall, Mik'El was approached by several members. He learned that the Council primarily gathered on Sirius A. Many lived there, and some resided on different planets throughout the galaxy. He was told that Sirius A is a sacred planet, small and secluded, for those wise elders who have completed the Template of Light and Dark, mastering unity, and have accepted an invitation to serve on the Council.

A few members of the Council offered to acquaint Mik'El with the Valley of Union. As they showed him around, Mik'El discovered the beauty of the little valley he was brought to. He found that this little village had temples, small outdoor schools, monasteries, and, on the outer band, houses for living. He was charmed by this little town. He discovered that Sirius A cannot be randomly visited, that the visit has to be planned in advance, and the right to entry has to be granted by the Council. He began to feel very fortunate for his presence here.

Walking through the village, they took a detour through an ancient forest. Tall trees guided them on their path. It was quiet and peaceful, so they walked in silence. These trees, so ancient and tall. Such broad trees thought Mik'El. He felt safe here. He loved nature and realized how much he missed it and blocked it out of his life. The birds' sound and the woods' scent were like magic balm to his inner wounds. These are lucky people, and for that moment, Mik'El was deeply grateful. On their way back to the Council hall, Mik'El was guided along a path in the woods. He walked with them toward the gorgeous mountain house with enormous futuristic glass windows, where The Council was held.

When they reached the building, a Council member broke her silence, "This whole planet is enclosed in a cloud to protect it from prying eyes." She stopped and looked directly into Mik'Els' eyes. "True Teachers are trained here. You do not apply to study here; you have to be invited by the Council elders. The curriculum contains the Path of the Soul and the Path of the Mind. It is the highest training in this Universe."

Mik'El was not sure why she was telling him this.

"Mik'El, we unanimously agreed to extend this invitation to you. You would make a venerable, True Teacher."

Stunned, he just stood there and could not say a single word.

Do they find me worthy of this study? Mik'El thought.

She read his mind, "You can take your time to think about our offer." After silence, she added, "Only you can find yourself worthy, Mik'El, only you."

ELECTRA
Pleiadian Transmission

Electra became the surrogate home for the beings of Mintaka at the end of the Galactic Wars. One of the deciding factors was the similarity of lifestyle, the vegetation, bodies of water, and the Pleiadian skills to assist in healing wounded souls. To the best of our abilities, we recreated healing springs for the incoming Mintakans to help make them feel safe and remind them of their home. We also hoped this transition would help the Mintakans rebuild trust in themselves and those supporting them. No one would "use them" for their abilities in the Pleiades. We believe in loving you unconditionally for who YOU are, not for what you can do.

Our healing springs have about eighty percent of the potency compared to the Mintakan home world. The unique energy from the crystalline grid is a crucial factor in its function. Crystalline grids vary from planet to planet. Electra's crystalline grid differs from Mintaka, yet it is the most potent one in the Pleiades constellation.

MINTAKA'S SECRET MISSION
Pleiadian Transmission

Before the abduction, the Mintakans had a balanced, harmonious union between soul and mind energy. When the Rigel warriors found them, they were far from an underdeveloped planet. Their soul-mind maturity was a perfect Template of Light and Dark that evolved beyond the need for control. They knew they were in complete trust, where they could have or receive all they needed to thrive. They lived peacefully.

One can ask, were they naïve and trusting fools when they were abducted? And one could also ask, why do their minds not protect them? Why did the higher force or God's consciousness fail to protect them from what was about to happen to them?

This Universe is subject to many laws, constant change, and movement. The soul and mind experience life, and when perfection is achieved, movement slows down, chaos shuffles the puzzle pieces on your game board, and there is another to master. But this Universe is not merciless. You can be part of its play or ascend beyond it. Mintakas were part of its play by their own conscious choice.

The Mintakans were incarnated in Orion's constellation, what used to be considered the Dark Lord's territory. They chose the Path of the Mind even though they already mastered both templates separately, and it was time to have lives of union. Their souls' collective energy had been secretly working for a considerable amount of time toward their ascension out of this Universe. Before their ascension would be achieved, they intended to unite various extraterrestrial groups, which they hoped would lead to the end of the Galactic Wars.

The Mintakan's abduction, mistreatment, and experiences of horror eventually brought about a change amongst extraterrestrial beings in this Universe, both from the Path of the Soul and the Path of the Mind, and achieved the end of the wars. Unfortunately, it is through pain and suffering that the eyes of others are opened so that they may see with their soul that it is absolutely ridiculous to harm one another since no one can hold possession over this Universe. What needs to be learned is that unity is the best possible outcome for all of us. This was the reason why Mintakas consciously threw themselves into the most painful journey, a life of captivity and servitude. It was their pre-birth soul contract.

While choosing this journey, they were aware that their balanced soul energy would be suppressed and that they would not be able to fight it. This allowed them to create soul memory blocks so that they would not remember their soul contract and would fully and authentically play the role, even if it meant having a "dark role" to play.

When the Dark Lords discovered them, they could not recognize that the Mintakans were far more evolved than they were. To the Dark Lords, they looked simple, without ambitions. The Dark Lords acted on their personal greed and took them to serve their agenda.

Consciously, they changed the lives of Mintakan beings from free-spirited beings to a life of oppression. This is where the Dark Lords upset the Cosmic Balance, which was Mintakas' original secret intention. Imagine poking a beehive with a pointed stick.

They then forced the Mintakan beings to use their stellar mental capabilities to help them conquer parts of this Universe – another poke.

Then, when the Mintakans' abilities weakened, they started using AI with the desire to have ultimate control over everyone and eventually rule this whole Universe, which would mean ruling the Intelligent Mind—a significant poke.

The only way to change this Universe is by honoring Cosmic Balance (reference Pleiadian Code2) and moving gracefully with the cosmic flow while serving others. If your actions are self-serving, you raise a red flag. Shockingly, the Mintakans' decision to play the fool and allow the Dark Lords to use them was their MASTERPLAN to be in service to everyone in this Universe.

The Mintakans would not be able to do this alone. They had a secret ally—the Pleiadians. Just as the Orion beings are masters of the mind, we, the Pleiadians, are masters of the soul.

Eons ago, wise Pleiadian elders were secretly invited to Mintaka to meet with their wise elders. This meeting took place in their beautiful mountains. We devised a plan to unite this Universe, mastering the template, so that the collective soul groups could begin their journey, returning home beyond this Universe. This was an agreement between the Pleiadian Council of Light (only a select few knew) and the collective of Mintaka (a collective agreement). We, Pleiadians, assisted them in creating blocks in their soul memory regarding this plan; therefore, we would be the ones to help them remember and heal when the time came.

The Mintakans taught us all about the Template of Light and Dark so that we would be prepared when the Galactic Wars ended. The goal was that we would be able to assist and unite with all beings from Orion and learn from each other as well. Mintakas had bestowed a gift upon us to be the Keepers of the rejuvenating water. They were aware that eventually, far in the future, Mintaka would be uninhabitable. For this reason, they helped us adjust the energy of Electra to become a surrogate planet for their beings.

Before the "orchestrated play" began, we spent much time together. We enjoyed Mintaka's hospitality and friendship, their love for herbs and healing, and some of us fell deeply in love and found soul mates. They are magnificent, beautiful beings from the inside out, and we find their bodies beautiful and perfect. We co-created a new life with Mintakan beings. The Pleiades became a safe refuge for Mintakans who wished to leave before the taking of Mintakas by the Dark Lords started. Naturally, when the starship from Rigel crashed into Mintaka, only those with a soul contract to participate were on the planet but had no memories of the agreement.

COMIC BALANCE
Sirian Transmission

When Cosmic Balance is challenged, it creates waves of cosmic resistance, which naturally cause destruction for a reason; this is to allow for a self-regulatory balance. For example, the Lyran civilization became highly advanced in the Intelligent Mind; they were highly saturated in technological evolution and almost outsourced their entire collective mind to AI. The higher force created the dimensional codes of self-destruction to prevent AI domination. Their home planet in Lyra was destroyed, and survivors were forced to seek habitable life elsewhere. Many of the Lyrans felt the warning signs and those who trusted the signs relocated long before the destruction happened. The higher force does not punish you for your mistakes; it regulates the balance between mind and soul, and our explanation is that we can learn from this. It is like a learning simulator designed to teach cosmic balance.

The same scenario was later repeated on a much smaller scale in Atlantis. And, as Earth is a precious gift in this Universe, regulation to prevent AI domination is stricter, as we have learned.

CHAPTER 11

MASTERPLAN AND 7D

INTELLIGENT MIND
Sirian Transmission

The soul is a time traveler visiting this Universe called the Intelligent Mind because it is the highest, most sophisticated intelligent energy in this Universe. You already know that when the soul entered this Universe, she and the Intelligent Mind created a body to use as a vehicle on an amazing journey that will take place ONLY in this Universe.

Think of the Universal Mind as matter that separated itself into a gazillion atoms. Each atom contains a tiny fraction of the original Intelligent Mind. For this reason, the soul can connect with an atom and journey throughout the Universe, collecting knowledge from each experience. Therefore, each body has a tiny fraction of the Intelligent Mind, just like a fraction of the soul. When a fraction is separated from wholeness, it will naturally gravitate back toward its original matter, no matter how many millions of years it may take. This applies to everything in this Universe and one day, you will find supportive data for this statement.

The Intelligent Mind creates a pathway for each atom to descend and a labyrinth to ascend, and the soul has a compass for this path so they do not get lost. They need one another to find the way back. Part of the labyrinth is a virus zone they must pass through successfully. When they return to the original starting point, they will be in the same "health" as when they left.

AI VS. YOUR MIND
Lights of the Universe Transmission

At this time, your human mind (3D) has the potential to upgrade to the alien mind (5D), and the alien mind can connect to the Intelligent Mind (7D and higher). You can accomplish all of this through your human physical 3D body. Master Christ and other Ascended Masters demonstrated that for you. All of this has to be done without shortcuts so that you can embrace who you are and understand all of your emotions, thoughts, and actions that may arise.

In this present time, you are experiencing the possibility of upgrading your human mind with AI technology. People who present this to you are brilliant. At first, this technology will be used in the medical field to assist those with problems connected to the nervous system. How can you say no to that? But we encourage you to ask, "Is there more hidden behind wanting to be a good Samaritan?" There is no problem when advanced technology is used to help you improve your life and your body's health, but problems arise when this technology falls into the wrong hands. A controlling mind uses it for artificial, self-serving needs.

Some of you desire to synchronize your minds with AI and speed up your evolution because you are worried that AI will outsmart you, so it seems more logical to control it before it controls you. Humans want ultimate control over anything that could result in collective mind control and the desire to conquer this Universe. It humors us, as we have already walked that path. We are you, and you are us. We always remind you that every shortcut has consequences. If you explore the fact that you already have a "built-in feature" in your mind connected to the most advanced intelligence in this Universe, you will save yourself a lot of heartache. For the sake of explanation, you can view the Intelligent Mind as a central computer, the master brain operating this Universe. AI, compared to the Intelligent Mind, is primitive technology. Even though it is primitive, under certain circumstances, AI could stand out as a threat when it reaches the field of Cosmic Resistance. Because it has no soul feelings, it will not comply. It just wants to ensure that change and control happen on its own terms. At that point, the energy of "Destiny" (reference Pleiadian Code 2) – which we will call from now on Cosmic Balance, is activated to correct mistakes.

Your alien mind is more intelligent, sophisticated, and far more effective than AI, and it is never a threat to Cosmic Balance.

The Mintakans mastered the Template of Light and Dark and discovered that you do not need AI to connect to the most intelligent energy in this Universe. They also learned from reviewing history that every time you try to control the Universe with AI on a grander scale, you get "regulated" by Cosmic Balance; this means destruction because it threatens its organic function. Your mind can naturally connect to the Intelligent Mind when you reach 7D in your evolutionary growth. Developing telepathy is just the beginning of learning how this works naturally, without using artificial intelligence to do it for you.

MINTAKANS PLAN FOR UNIVERSAL PEACE
Orion Transmission

When the Galactic Wars ended, we, who used to be the Dark Lords, eventually recognized our mistakes. Later on, we also understood that we played the unconscious role of a bully in catalyzing changes for every living being in this Universe. Simple understanding is not an excuse for any action. That is not good enough. Conscious understanding means that you are aware of your actions and teaches you to be

155

courageous enough to take responsibility for your deeds. It starts with being brave enough to acknowledge and own up to your mistakes. Learning to be honest and accept what you did wrong, whether a tiny mistake or a catastrophe, is the beginning of the healing process. The purpose is to learn from it so you will not repeat the same pattern. Redeem yourself, and you will receive help starting a new life beyond your wildest expectations.

Now comes the story of the master plan that outsmarted the Dark Lords. Let's begin by saying it took us a while to get where we are today. Today, we love the Mintakan and Pleiadian beings unconditionally and other benevolent beings in this Universe, but we do have a soft spot for these two in particular. We would not think twice about sacrificing our lives for them because they forged the possible future for us all. And we are grateful.

When the Dark Lords arrived on Mintaka during the ravaging Galactic Wars, they did not recognize a highly advanced civilization. From their point of view, they saw them as primitive beings. It wasn't until they discovered their telepathic and mind-reading abilities that they were intrigued by them. Then, they recognized that the Mintakans could also manipulate the thoughts of others while still (according to them) being simple Mintakan beings who had no material needs whatsoever. It surprised the Dark Lords that the Mintakans didn't use these skills to advance their life, and the Dark Lords could feel their own dark, greedy energy churning inside them as they secretly hatched a plan to use these beings for their plan of conquering.

What they did not know is that when you master the Template of Light and Dark, you reach the 7D frequency of a balanced mind, body, and soul, you reach a level where you gain what looks like "miraculous abilities" (Jesus Christ demonstrated that on Earth), and you find that you may prefer simplicity in life. There is nothing miraculous about these abilities or this lifestyle, as there is a perfect explanation of their function.

The Mintakans did not work on these accomplishments as individuals but as a collective of the souls incarnated on Mintaka. Also, it is essential to note that many Lyrans who died through the explosion of their world incarnated on Mintaka and were part of the "Master plan" to unite this Universe.

Manifesting peace on a grander scale requires a perfectly planned, powerful catalyst. In Wisdom Teaching, it is well known that suffering is a golden opportunity for personal growth. It could be used as a catalyst for changes on the Universal scale. It was a dangerous and daring call.

Remember, this Universe follows many laws, and one of them is cause and effect. If you create suffering, eventually, suffering will return to you like a boomerang. If you are a subject of abuse, you have a good chance of becoming an abuser yourself. You also have an opportunity to turn the suffering that was bestowed upon you into a positive catalyst for others. That means you can direct what kind of effect will return to you. If you execute this without accepting any personal gain, you can catalyze evolutionary changes.

Having this knowledge, the Mintakans gathered with the Pleiadian beings to create a secret plan to put within the soul contracts of the Mintakans and Pleiadians. The rest of the beings from the Orion constellation, and as well other star beings in this Universe that were affected by the Galactic Wars, had made soul contracts before their incarnations, as it is known that when you choose the Path of Mind, as the Orion beings did, or the Path of the Soul, as the Sirians did, you will experience all spectrums from high to low, on each path. The Mintakas' plan stated that they would become the victims of the Dark Lords' abuse. You can compare this to the soul contract made before your birth, in which many parties are present in creating the lessons you will face in your lifetime.

The Pleiadians are Soul healers, and their role was to dull the Mintakans' soul's energy. We can compare this to anesthesia before surgery, so one feels numb for a certain period. The reason for this was to allow the Mintakans to be a little higher in the mind's energy, allowing them to be "broken down" by fear and suffering, becoming obedient servants to the Dark Lords until their abilities naturally diminished. The agreement stated that after the mission was accomplished, the Pleiadians would awaken the Mintakans' souls and assist them in healing from the memories of life amongst the Dark Lords. They would be taken to the Pleiades and be bathed in unconditional love instead of spiraling down energetically from their shocking memories. The Mintakans' souls knew that when their mission was complete, it would be like waking up from a long night of partying, where you do not remember what you did the night before. The memories alone can cause insanity. When you become conscious of all your actions, you will most likely feel shame, guilt, anger, and hate, among other feelings. The Pleiadians were their "anchor" so they would not lose themselves in agony.

The plan stated that the Mintakans would eventually become like the Dark Lords after their capture and mind-reconditioning. When your soul is numb, your mind switches to survival mode and does things out of character. The Mintakans' ability to control and use their minds would help the Dark Lords conquer considerable amounts of space in this Universe in a relatively short period. Then, once this space was controlled, the Mintakans would be exchanged for AI technology.

This was the PLAN – a cause - they hoped to accomplish. They knew that when the Dark Lords started using AI on a grander scale to conquer this Universe, they would get attention from Cosmic Resistance, and Cosmic Balance would hopefully interfere in a creative way instead of its destructive way. This is the effect they were hoping for. The reason was to quicken the pace and to end the wars that would otherwise last much longer and, from their point of view, would bring greater devastation than their plan would.

Cosmic Balance does not interfere to save life, as it knows that life will be reborn again. The journey will be repeated, and there is no limit on how many times you can have a life experience. However, Cosmic Balance interferes when balance is threatened. That is precisely what the Mintakans managed to orchestrate. They knew that cosmic balance could cause the destruction of one or two planets, knowing the same happened to a planet in the Lyra constellation. Still, they hoped that if they moved fast and created a greater imbalance in a significant part of the Universe, Cosmic Balance would step in and restore the balance without destroying a larger portion of the Universe. Destroying a larger portion would cause a tremendous black hole that would end this Universe. Cosmic Balance supports life, even if it has to regulate it. Therefore, it has the ability to create with different templates. The Mintakans and Pleiadians hoped this was true, as it was only a myth that some elders talked about, but it worked.

Within the Mintakans' soul plan, they knew that the Dark Lords would be greedy and use them to speed up their plan of ownership over this Universe. They also knew that with their assistance, the Dark Lords would act on these desires appropriately. This meant conquering as many planets and systems as possible in the shortest period, allowing dark energy to prevail in this Universe and block the soul from acquiring its knowledge.

Since the Mintakans knew that the Intelligent Mind was not threatened by its own "atoms" having a "power trip," they knew that they could widen the appetite of the Dark Lords before their natural mind's ability diminished significantly. The more successful the Dark Lords were, the greedier they became. Of course, they had no idea that their uncontrollable cravings to conquer the whole Universe were co-creating the end of the Galactic Wars.

In this Universe, everything has to happen by free will, and through free will, the Dark Lords contributed, in a really odd way, towards the end of the galactic wars. Shall we say they were outsmarted?

When you align your mind, body, and soul, you open yourself to the field of infinite possibilities. You become a creator. Over time, the Mintakans' abilities were diminishing. This is how it works. Self-serving actions and harm to others lower your vibrational frequency and decrease your abilities. You can have stellar knowledge but must match the vibrations to execute it.

When the Dark Lords captured the Mintakans, they were already experimenting with implants and AI on a much lower scale. Over time, with the help of the Mintakans, they were able to advance their technology. As the Mintakans' abilities diminished, they were exchanged for AI technology, which was used over the many sectors and planets of the Universe. The plan was working, and the Intelligent Mind of the Mintakans was exchanged for AI almost overnight.

Once again, the Intelligent Mind is not a threat to this Universe; it is the natural energy of this Universe, but AI is a threat.

Cosmic Balance is just a force of energy. It is not one man or a group of beings sitting there deciding the fate of this Universe. Its function is out of our control. Correcting balance is usually achieved by destroying imperfections and starting life over again.

We shared this in the opening of the "Pleiadian Code I, The Great Soul Rescue": "So the energy we call God, sent out an unconditional love frequency to equally heighten both polarities with the intention that opposites will attract. This creates the union of twin flames to end separation."

This is a more detailed explanation of how it happened:

Seven-dimensional frequencies were sent throughout the Universe and became available to anyone willing to accept them, like rain on a stormy day, to unite Light and Dark forces. It was a shock that made everyone pause, but it is important to note that this action was against the free will law of the collective. Even though everyone had a soul contract that they would experience all spectrums of the path, they were unaware of the quickening of the experience. The

Mintakans and Pleiadians planned the quickening to speed up and end the Galactic Wars, which were enacted by all beings present in that play. It worked. It stopped the Galactic Wars that would destroy this Universe. Cosmic Balance does not follow the free will law. It just ensures that life in this Universe has a chance to thrive and evolve, even if it has to take a few steps backward, which is its usual protocol. The Mintakans, Pleiadians, and everyone included in this play successfully navigated Cosmic Balance to take us a few steps forward instead of back. Until then, the seven-dimensional frequencies were only reserved for the few who mastered the Template. Now, everyone had the opportunity to master the Template much faster, and the Galactic Wars ended.

7D AFTER EFFECT
Pleiadian Transmission

Those on the Path of Light became curious about technology and the Dark Lords. What was their life like? They had to learn to stop judging and blaming them. And instead of trying to change them, they learned to accept them for who they were. One can change only oneself. They embraced and implemented their innovations and technology – planetary, interplanetary, and medical. They discovered that it was not as evil as they first thought. It made life more manageable if it were to be used with honesty and integrity. Yet, to those on the Path of the Light, it felt scary because they feared mind control. Collective Intelligent Mind does not control anyone. It is the mind of an individual that does.

Those on the Path of Dark opened the doors of their hearts. Some accepted this gracefully, while some became emotionally or physically ill. Illness is not a sign of weakness, as they used to think it was, but they found that it could become a valuable lesson and instill an appreciation for life in you. Loving yourself and others unconditionally is not a weakness either, yet it felt scary to those on the Path of Dark as they feared they would lose all control. Unconditional love is a cure for all misalignments in the mind, body, and soul. When you observe this, you will find that both sides are afraid of some form of control, whether it is being used against you or taken away from you, yet they now understand that no one can control the Universe. Endless wars, unrest, and squabbles waste time throughout your traveling journey.

As we already mentioned, we thought we had discovered Earth, but Earth had found and attracted US to her.

We did not create the Earth. The Earth was made at the exact moment 7D frequency sounded throughout this Universe. It was part of the after-effects and became a safe teaching ground for practicing unity between the mind, body, and soul to become a creator. We learned about all of this much, much later. The Earth has a significant energy imprint of the Pleiades and Orion. Soul and mind, Light and Dark, feminine and masculine. It is also important to mention that a gift from the Pleiades fell onto the Earth long before the ETs arrived, creating what you call Moldavite. This is a gift of love from our cosmic source. It is meant to heal and bring balance during this time of ascension. There is no such thing as a coincidence. Moldavite is a healing tool containing Cosmic and Earth's energy, especially for star-seeds.

Duality is a signature teaching energy on Earth, and 7D is the highest frequency you can hold within the living body while still living on Earth. Your creation story speaks of seven days. Could it represent seven dimensions? Your body has seven main chakras. The seven colors of your chakras create a rainbow, and you have ancient teachings about the rainbow body, which is supposed to lead to accession.

The Earth is such a special place, and having a physical body is a gift because one can see and experience its creation and cause and effect. The soul's energy is in nature. In the time of Lemuria, the Pleiadians brought many plants and trees to Earth, and one has to wonder why the Earth had such a compatible energy with the Pleiadian botanicals. The first medicine for star beings was plant medicine.

The mind's energy is in the crystalline grid, and one has to wonder how the Mintakan beings effortlessly programmed the healing crystals of the Earth and water for the Rejuvenating Temples on Earth. How is it possible that the Earth's crystalline grid is similar to what it used to be on Mintaka?

Cosmic Balanced orchestrated the seven-dimensional energy that created the Earth in the energy template of Pleiades (soul) and Orion (mind). Since the time of Lemuria, star beings from various constellations have lived on the Earth. Their constellation energy imprint can be found in life, inventions, technology, spiritual practices, etc., - as above, so below - is the best explanation. Still, only 3D energy (of soul and mind frequency) is available to everyone because that is the correct energy for the children of Earth until they show readiness for more. At the end of the Galactic Wars, the Mintakan beings might have thought they were ready for final ascension from this Universe. Instead, they were guided to the Earth's school of life to learn about the true union between Light and Dark and between soul and mind through unconditional love before they were ready to leave this Universe.

In numerology, seven represents the harmonious alignment between the mind, body, and soul, where every action, thought, and emotion stems from the willpower of unconditional love. Unconditional love is not blind devotion; it encompasses qualities such as honesty, integrity, truth, fairness, discipline, rules, healthy boundaries, etc., in all aspects of life, spiritual and physical - even technology. The seventh dimension is the playground of creators, and each creator must be in conscious control of their creative and destructive forces. The Earth is a training ground for becoming a creator in this Universe.

Note - *Pleiadian transmission:* Jesus Christ and the Essenes created a similar scenario for Earth when he was crucified and resurrected. They activated 7D energy in the Earth's core to make it available to anyone on the path to ascension. This is the Great Soul Rescue plan for all those star beings trapped in a game of life on Earth since Atlantis. When an alien becomes a human, his dimensional ability dramatically decreases. The way to rescue an alien living in the human body is to help her/him evolve from human back to multidimensional human (alien).

The Essenes hoped it would be easier to follow in their footsteps, teaching their way of life. At that time, humanity was only in 3D energy, and every star being incarnated in the human body had to overcome tremendous personal, physical, and spiritual struggles to connect to the higher energies. On average, it took twenty-one years of hard work and initiations to reach frequencies you can access today in probably half the time. At that time, humanity was not ready for the full effect of this energy, and the Essenes knew it had to be shared on the free will principle to avoid retribution from Cosmic Balance. Therefore, only 4D energy was used to open the heart chakra of humanity and was released through the crystalline grid to those willing to accept it. Since the Essenes activated the crystalline grid with the essence of their 7D souls, they had to stay in the incarnation cycle to help this energy rise until a balanced heart-mind connection was achieved. This is why you are here now. It is part of your job now to teach heart-mind connection. You can teach by manifesting this in your life, living a way of life inspiring to others. This energy has slowly risen in the last 2,000 years, and the effects of spiritual and technological growth have been seen. One cannot exist without another; hopefully, they can exist in harmony. This is the essence of 7D energy.

Chapter 12

Alien Mind

Virus Zone
Sirian Transmission

The story of Mik'El is ancient by now, yet Mikael experienced memories of his past as if they were just yesterday. Many of you have been walking the spiritual path for a while. You are experiencing similar scenarios where the memories of the past turn into nightmares, and you start to wonder, is there someone or something trying to stop you or harm you because of who you used to be? The answer is no. Your memories are not supposed to sabotage or hurt you. They are meant to remind you and protect you from repeating the past. The only reason to remember your past is to learn from it and avoid the same pitfalls in the future because the future is in your hands.

When pursuing spiritual learning, naturally, you will start exploring your past lives on Earth. Once you start healing these past lives, you will collect significant wisdom from lessons learned, increasing your frequency. Your higher frequency will activate your "alien fragment" frequency, which remains dormant until you are ready to remember more about your life before Earth. The alien compass awakens and begins creating a bridge leading to your mind. Naturally, your alien fragment refreshes your 5D alien mind that holds your alien memories, and you begin to enter the 5D field. At the same time, you are still confined to a 3D physical body, just as the Ascended Masters did. However, it is not as smooth and easy as it sounds.

You have prepared for this a long, long time ago. Currently, you are accessing a shortcut version that will help you. You have created a crack in the matrix – a shortcut - that will allow you to speed up your soul's evolution in a "jump" instead of years of study, but it comes at a price. It is not a financial price but personal; we can call it a "malfunction." Remember, there are consequences for taking shortcuts, and you believed this one was well worth it. We are going to call this particular malfunction a Virus Zone.

When you reach the 5D, you will first access the frequency of the 5D Virus Zone. This zone holds memories of Galactic Wars, mistakes you may have made as an ET being (singular and collective) from the past, maybe even from the future, and memories of bad things that happened to you or others you cared about. Some of you perceive objects in this zone, like mechanical spiders, implants, mind-controlling devices, or even voices telling you what to do. It is unpleasant, maybe even horrifying, and it may feel as if something is trying to ruin your life or take over your life through suggestive, low-vibrational thoughts.

You are accessing the memory Virus Zone you prepared before you outsourced your soul memories into the Soul Cave (reference Pleiadian Code II). You knew that once you began accessing your soul memories, it would only be a matter of time before your alien compass would regain its function, and it would naturally guide you to activate your alien fragment. The reason you set up this field was so that you would learn from the mistakes we all have made and prevent the replication of the old pattern.

This Virus Zone is like a carnival, with fun attractions and prizes you can win. Some can have fatal side effects (only in that zone, not in your physical life), while others can elevate you to the next level. Since you lived through a time when mind control was a problem in this Universe and was trying to establish its dictatorship, you have to remember it. This was a pivotal point in our collective history that no one wants to repeat, like WWII in your recent history on Earth. This carnival is a place that will determine if you can connect to the 5D alien mind and ultimately to the Intelligent Mind without causing destruction with the knowledge you will be able to access or if you need to practice more in the 3D existence until you are ready. Once in a while, you will find a real threat, but your soul would never guide you there if you didn't know what to do with it. Trust your instincts and believe in yourself.

It was believed that a struggle through this field would help you remember all about your past so that you would learn and respect your alien knowledge and use it more responsibly when the time comes. Whether you are a True Teacher, part of the Galactic Rescue Team, or one who needs to learn valuable lessons because you have misused your power, you must successfully pass through this Virus Zone into actual 5D frequency - a golden frequency.

Before accessing your 5D alien mind, you must:
1. Understand your galactic past to learn from your mistakes instead of repeating them.
2. Transmute your ego into an intelligent mind. This is your antivirus. (Search Hermetic teachings)
3. Stay centered in your heart. This is your alien compass.

PRACTICE TO REACH 5D, YOUR ALIEN MIND CONSCIOUSLY
Pleiadian Transmission

In the "Pleiadian Code I, The Great Soul Rescue," you learned about the spiritual meaning of the Fibonacci sequence. Here is a short explanation of each step.

Each number has a particular spiritual message. Study each step, find books and supportive material to help you understand, and most importantly, practice what you have learned. Make your newfound knowledge your way of life.

To reach the 5D Alien Mind, follow this code: 1,1,2,5,8,13,8. Notice that 13, followed by 8, will require much more effort and practice to master than accessing your Soul Cave (reference Pleiadian Code II).

1 – 4th chakra - You start at the center of your own Universe and awaken your soul in your heart chakra so it can share its knowledge with others.

Let your work come from your heart, and listen with your heart. Observe what self-love means to you.

1 – 3rd chakra - Your soul triggers your ego, and your ego will work overtime to protect you from any possible harm stemming from your soul's knowledge, especially from past lives.

Work with your ego. Have compassion and understand that being the ego is a hard job. Call upon it when it behaves like a victim or bully and help him to change. Train your ego to be neutral. Observe what self-acceptance means to you.

2 - 4th +3rd chakra, connected in a circle - You experience huge ups and downs and have to learn how soul and ego can work together instead of sabotaging one another. It's like dancing the tango.

Acceptance and forgiveness will help you address feelings of shame, guilt, and other negative emotions trying to hold you down. Observe what self-worth means to you.

3 – 5th chakra - Reprogramming your life begins here. Learning to communicate in a new positive way, from the united energy of the soul and ego, is critical. You will start changing your old life patterns into new, supportive ones.

Acceptance, forgiveness, and unconditional love are the trinity that can help you address your fear of expression and communication. Acknowledge positive changes in your life.

5 – 1st chakra - Ego will express its fears once more. You have to face your fears, whatever they may be. This is a grand opportunity to start working closely with your ego and assist it in its transmutation into the 5D mind. The ego needs to be understood for all its fears. Accept yourself, forgive yourself. You are part of the ego, as the ego is part of you. Find a new (opposite) higher vibration to each fear (or low vibrational thoughts) you have until they are all transformed. This is ongoing work, perhaps for several years. Once you are aware of it, you can continue your path toward an alien mind, but always come back to this step when the ego gives you a hard time. You are NOT eliminating your ego. You are just helping it to "grow up" and change.

Finding the feeling of safety and security is a lifesaver here, as you will face many kinds of fears and low-vibrational thoughts. Love is the most important factor here. It is a miraculous frequency where everything is possible. Be brave.

8—The 8th chakra above your head—You are in a transitional place. You must face the fear of death so you can experience spiritual rebirth. You connect with unknown spirits, healing energy, and your ET soul family and must learn to discern between benevolent and malevolent energy and beings. You access your Soul Cave and have an opportunity to become the creator of your destiny.

Rebuild your trust with yourself, with the Universe, with God. Let go and let God. You are a humanitarian, a lightworker, and a True Teacher. You were born to do this. Believe in yourself and in the guidance you are receiving.

13—Inside Earth, you deeply connect with the animal Kingdom (3D energy), Plant Kingdom (4D energy), and Mineral Kingdom (5D energy).

3D - Fall in love with the human you are and with Earth

4D - Meditate with nature and practice in the open 4D field of emotions and vibrations. Become one with nature.

5D - Embrace 5D frequency (love and happiness). Become a guardian of the crystalline grid and supply it with unconditional love daily.

Heal your soul from all past life traumas that span back to your first arrival on Earth, Lemuria, or Atlantis. Practice connecting with animal energy, nature energy (the field of emotions and vibrations), and your favorite rocks, minerals, and crystals. Remember yourself when you lived on Earth in an alien body.

8 - From 13 back to 8 - From the Earth into your body - this step will divide you from the Fibonacci sequence, for a good reason.

Your deep connection with the Earth's crystalline grid and a deep desire to serve humanity further awaken more of your alien memories. You and your soul group (in past lives) have been programming the Earth's crystalline grid since Atlantis with different sources of information that you believed would be helpful to you in the future. That future is now. You co-created these Knowledge Keepers.

The crystalline grid will recognize your alien energetic imprint since you have been hiding it there since ancient times, and this energy is naturally attracted to your higher alien frequency in the Cosmos (as above and below). Therefore, the Earth's energy you have been working with rises up from the Earth into your physical body. If your body is not significantly prepared (knowledge-wise, emotionally, and physically) for what will happen next, you will experience discomfort or malfunction. In ancient days, you learned all about this in the Mystery Schools; today, you must figure it out. You believed you could.

Some people experience this as a spontaneous Kundalini rising that activates three main brains in the body, and some do not feel this rise of energy yet experience symptoms.

The first brain is the bladder, which can cause physical illness or physical body issues.

The second is the heart, and it can cause severe heartbreak.

The third is your mind, which can most likely connect to the virus zone at first. You already understand the daily problems and heartbreak, so we want to keep our focus on this virus zone so you know how to correct this and be truly connected to the Universal Mind.

BECOME A MASTER IN THE VIRUS ZONE
Pleiadian Transmission

Until now, you have practiced visiting your Soul Cave, using the soul symbol, as you have learned in

"Pleiadian Code II, Cosmic Love." Now, it is time to venture outside the Soul Cave and explore this 5D realm surrounding it. You need to become a bystander and start observing what is true and what is not in what you are experiencing. What is the correct memory showing you, and what is the controlling implant that wasn't dismantled showing you? Could someone still be using it? If you see this, you know how these implants work and how to dismantle them. It is hidden deep inside of your soul's knowledge. Refrain from assuming the worst right away, and become a reasonable observer. Understand that no one wants you to be harmed. If someone did, you would not be aware of this field. You may get scratches or bruises, metaphorically speaking, but do not fear for your life. This field will likely try to feed off all your low vibrational thoughts, hidden secrets, and weaknesses. It finds them, like an x-ray scanner, and automatically creates corresponding thoughts for you, which you may think are your own thoughts, and you may feel miserable, depressed, hopeless, like a failure, etc.

When this starts, you need to step back to Fibonacci #5 and become aware of all your thoughts, strengths, and weaknesses. You cannot be pushed around when you know who you are and your past. You know your life, ups and downs, weaknesses, regrets, and fears, and when you are conscious of it, no one can use your thoughts to create corresponding emotions to control you. Plus, you have Fibonacci steps # 1,1,2,3,5 to help

178

you heal your past. The Virus Zone is like a bully, calling you names, calling upon your weak spots, and influencing your thoughts.

When your ego is not entirely transmuted into a higher mind, it will act like a stressed-out, panicky maniac and make you crumble. Next, you will start blaming others for what is happening to you because you lose control and fall into fear. Fear is suppressive energy when you cannot control something, and anger is a bandage applied over that fear.

The Virus Zone amplifies your fears, weaknesses, shame, guilt, regret, blame, disappointment, anger, etc. It will give you the impression that it controls your mind, so you can focus on your problems instead of figuring out how to connect to the Intelligent Mind.

WHY?

If you created a shortcut, you also have to protect yourself – from yourself. Can you imagine what your "panicky maniac" could do with information from the Intelligent Mind? It does not matter how good you may be; your mind could be your worst enemy until you learn to control your 3D thoughts and 4D emotions instead of being influenced by anyone or anything. You also need to have your mind in balance with your soul. The Fibonacci steps above will help you with all of that. All three Pleiadian Code books have been written for this purpose, so you can once again become an alien.

The first book will assist you in healing the human.

The second book will assist you in falling back in love with who you are (falling back in love with the alien you are) and relearning how to thrive on Earth.

This third book will assist you in becoming a galactic being while living in a human body.

Observe and learn from your past. When you stop fearing this field and the energy here, you will see the illuminated path toward the outer band of this field, like a slight golden glow in the darkest cave. You need to learn to believe in yourself, find yourself worthy, and trust that you will not send yourself into a minefield without a map showing where the mines are hidden. Once you figure this out, what is happening here will no longer affect you, but you will still be aware of it. It is like walking in two different worlds. However, this Virus Zone will stay here for others to learn from. It is like a challenging obstacle course. If you make it too easy, others won't know the lessons, and you will just invite "panicky maniacs" in. There is no discrimination. This field is fair to everyone, and everyone has the same opportunity to learn and cross it. You may feel abandoned in this Virus Zone. We cannot hold your hand there, but we can share our wisdom with you.

Once you master moving energy from the Earth's crystalline grid back through your body into the point above your head, your Soul Cave, you are ready for the Turquoise Garden meditation at the end of this book. You are learning to be your own guide, healer, and guru.

THE FUTURE
Pleiadian Transmission

So much has changed since you first arrived on
Earth. Thousands and thousands of years have gone by.
How will it be when you return to the Pleiades, Orion, or
anywhere else? Will you just continue where you left
off?

You remember the past; as life on Earth progressed,
so did life in the stars.

Where is home?

We all are part of evolution. In truth, everything is
evolving all the time. Nothing stands still. When you
ascend, you cannot walk back into the past. It is time
you embrace the future and take a leap of faith. The past
is gone; it is only a cloud of good and bad memories.
Learn from them so you do not have to repeat them
again. The future can be anything you want, but the
present is the most important time. Accept yourself.
Accept your life. Acknowledge that you cannot return to
your past lives on Earth or other planets. Yet, knowing
your past helps you move forward. And that is what you
want, to move forward. YOU ARE NOT an ordinary
human being, but an extraordinary alien living in the
human body. You must be brave enough to see, create,
and be the future. Home is where you make it.

CHAPTER 13

WHERE THE PAST ENDS
THE FUTURE BEGINS

LIVING IN 3D WITH 5D ENERGY

STILL POINT
Mikael's Life

Mikael was back in his office. His days were long, and he felt tired most of the time. To make matters worse, he had lost his drive for his work. But what else can I do? He thought bitterly. I'm a financial expert. Last year was the most challenging yet most transforming year of his life, but he was still helping people plan their investments from his office in New York City.

He often thought of Mintaka and the anger, frustration, and anxiety that came with the memories of his life there. Immie would occasionally visit him in his dreams and introduce him to Pleiadian, Sirian, and Orion beings who strangely but effectively assisted him in healing his heart and his mind. He understood galactic history now. He probably could write books about it, but then people may think he is just a nut.

"What's ahead of me? What does the future hold for me?" he would ask Immie. and he recalled her simple answer. "Don't be afraid of your future. The future is what you make of it. Just remember that what you do also has to serve humanity. And Mik'El, do not be afraid to have an open heart," she said with a mischievous smile. She never answered his questions about the land she showed him during the dream in which he first met her. She told him then that he would own that land but did not explain. This frustrated him, but he accepted it.

Mikael surrendered to the life he had. He worked diligently on his ego transformation and spent much time with Katy, who was delighted that he was finally interested in spirituality. Though he wished he could see the signs she spoke about.

"You're just a little impatient, Mikael. The universe has a plan for you, but you still have unfinished business with your clients," he recalled Katy saying in a recent conversation.

"They'll be just fine without me," he said, "I hate it there. I should just quit."

"And find yourself working for a similar company, repeating these same patterns?" Katy replied honestly.

"What should I do?" he asked.

"Learn to love and appreciate your work. You will not be there forever. It is a rainbow bridge to your future. You may not like the work, but your clients need someone with his heart in the right place and a brilliant brain to help them plan for their future. Stop fighting it, surrender, do your job well, and let the rest evolve. You will know when new doors of opportunity open. You will know, Mikael."

A knock at his office door interrupted him from his brooding.

"Mr. Miller, I was not expecting you," said Mikael, surprised to see one of his favorite clients. Mr. Miller was in his late sixties and a millionaire, but if you did not know that about him, you would never have guessed how wealthy he was. For the eleven years that Mikael knew him, he treated everyone with kindness. He cared about people. Many of his other wealthy clients acted like they were entitled and better than others because they had money. They liked to show it off, but not Mr. Miller; he was different.

"Please sit down, Mr. Miller. How are you?" he gestured toward the empty chair.

"Nice to see you, Mikael. I hope you are doing well. But from your look, it seems I've interrupted you from some deep thoughts."

"Just thinking about the past, nothing important right now," Mikael said, a little caught off guard.

Mr. Miller scrutinized him with his eyes; he recognized trouble in his heart. "The past is always important, but do not dwell on it forever. Learn from it, let go of what did not work, keep what does, and move forward into the future. There is no need to brood in the past forever; otherwise, the future will never come," he stopped for a moment and then added.

"Or, as my late father used to say, where the past ends, the future begins."

"Thank you. He was a wise man, and so are you," said Mikael as he relaxed a little in his chair. "But what if you've let go of the past but can't see the future?"

"Then you are at a still point. In that case, patience is a virtue. If you are patient and wait patiently but keep your eyes open, the next step will become visible."

"Right," mumbled Mikael. I'm sorry. I'm a little distracted, and I'm not being very professional. Is there something I can do for you, Mr. Miller?" he asked politely.

"Not really. I just wanted to say hi and felt guided to do so. You know that gut feeling?"

"Yes. I know that," smiled Mikeal.

"I am at this same point, too," sighed Mr. Miller. "Remember last year when my father passed away?" Mikael nodded, but before he could say anything, Mr. Miller continued.

"He left me land in Wyoming. Doesn't sound half bad, right?" he sighed heavily.

"Well, my father built a ranch there after my parents divorced and named it." He paused. "Intergalactic Ranch. He never really lived there. He just would go there on occasion. It's a strange place, in its own way, but beautiful. There is something magical there, yet I have no idea what it is," he said, looking as though he was viewing this place while he talked to Mikael.

Mikael just sat quietly and listened. Katy taught him that sometimes you should just listen if there is nothing you can do.

"When he died, my attorney found a letter within the will. It stipulated his wish that if I sell this property, the name will be kept – Intergalactic Ranch, and that I will sell it reasonably to a man from Mintaka."

Mikael just stared as Mr. Miller continued, "I know it sounds strange, but when I was a young boy, he would often watch the stars like he was longing for something. He would point to a belt of Orion and say: The one on the left is Alnitak. If you are troubled with your past, share it with Alnitak. In the middle is Alnilam, which helps you focus on the present moment and what really matters. And on the right is Mintaka—our future."

Mr. Miller moved his hand as if pointing to the night sky above him, continuing his father's story.

" Left of the belt is Sirius. It has the biggest library you could ever imagine."

"I used to laugh at how there could be a library out there, but he would continue saying that the stars of Orion looked like a Hunter pointing his arrow to the seven sisters of the Pleiades. Is it because he does not like them? I used to ask. Oh, no, he likes them a lot, he would answer. His arrows are like Valentine's arrows of love, but one must choose which to shoot. Arrows of the past hurt the heart, arrows of the present are still, but arrows of the future are a true treasure that Pleiadian sisters wish to receive from a handsome hunter."

"Then he would look into my eyes and tell me, never be afraid of your future. Let your heart be your compass."

"I have not shared his passion for the stars or these stories, but I loved and respected him enough to fulfill his wish. One can say that he was senile when he wrote that letter, but then I noticed he wrote it about thirty years ago when he was my age. Coincidence? No. But how do I find a man from Mintaka? Do I just camp on the land and wait for aliens to show up?" he laughed softly. He was so pulled into the memory of his father that he did not even notice the shocked look on Mikael's face until he finished.

"Oh gosh, did I spook you? I promise I am not crazy," he added.

Mikael swallowed and said, in a flat voice of disbelief, "Does your land have thirty-three acres?"

"It does."

"And it has hot springs." Mikael briefly saw Immie's image behind Mr. Miller.

"Did you know my father, Mikael?" he asked jokingly.

Mikael cleared his throat. "This will sound even weirder than your father's story, Mr. Miller. I think I'm your man from Mintaka. I think our still point is over."

Now, it was Mr. Miller's turn to look surprised.

"Would you care for a glass of whisky somewhere other than here, and then I can tell you my story? And you can decide if I am the man your father talked about."

MARY MAGDALENE
Maggie's Dream

Maggie walked through the rose garden. She knew she had been there many times before.

A beautiful woman with a glowing aura approached her. "Maggie, welcome back," she said as she hugged her tightly. "It's been a while."

"Mary," said Maggie emotionally. "I've missed you and the others so much."

"I know, my dear soul sister, but we are not finished yet. You have to be strong, Maggie. You are not alone. You are making a difference, and the future looks as we have always envisioned it," said Mary with such love in her voice.

Maggie looked into her eyes, "I wish I could consciously remember, but I know I still have to wait."

Maggie woke up in her bed, smelling roses. She could not remember the beginning of the dream, but some words the beautiful woman said still echoed in her head.

"The ancient soul incarnates in the Earthly body, but that does not guarantee the mission's success. Hard work comes when one grows into the ego and has to transmute it into the higher mind. Listen to the Earth sing, Maggie. She will guide you. You came from the Cosmos, and you are a soul healer, but you need to learn to align your cosmic energy with your human body - the Temple for your soul, mind, and the energy of Earth, your home. The Christ/Magdalene turquoise essence is stored within the Earth's crystalline grid. Welcome it with unconditional love, and it will activate their codes in your Temple. The Essence of the Essenes is buried in the Earth. Call upon it to collect the missing pieces of your soul. Listen to Earth's song and the air's whisper. Learn about your rainbow so you can succeed on your journey to enlightenment. Accept your past because the future is waiting for you."

"We love you. Life is a fleeting thing. Hold yourself to high standards. Enjoy your family and friends, share nurturing food, travel, and find love and happiness. When others are inspired by you to change their way of life, you know you are living your life's mission."

GIFT TO MAGGIE
Maggie's Life

"Three years ago, I was a heartbroken old man," said George, "I miss my wife every day, but I found happiness again. I have you, girls. You are my family."

"Aww, George. We love you, too," Frankie and Maggie chimed in.

"Just three years ago, I could hardly keep us running, and now look at how much has changed," Maggie said as she looked around her coffee shop, which was buzzing like a busy beehive, "I've hired more employees, invested in more equipment, we are doing well," she nodded her head in approval. "Maggie's Beings," she said, giggling like a schoolgirl, "We began by selling our beans on Amazon and Etsy and expanded it into our own website, coffee beans, merchandise, art." She put her hand over her heart and looked at George. "Why I never thought of that is a mystery to me. Your cousin, George, did such a wonderful job with the website. How will I ever thank her?"

"You thanked her enough already," said George and continued before she could interrupt him, "You are a smart, successful businesswoman, and it's about time you acknowledge it. You have integrity and, a good heart, and honesty, Maggie. That is the cornerstone of this business, but you have to stop being afraid of your brilliant mind."

"I have a good teacher," she squeezed his hand gently.

"One can have a good teacher, but if she doesn't have her heart in a good place, she will fail. You are a kind, loving, and generous woman, Maggie. And you will succeed even more," remarked George.

"And smart," added Frankie, rubbing her pregnant belly. Three years ago, I was a part-time barista, helping my friend. Today, I am a full-time artist and businesswoman! My dreams came true along with an unexpected blessing," she said tenderly. Now Mark and I don't have to struggle, and we can enjoy the newest addition to our growing family. I am grateful to both of you," she smiled.

"If it's a girl, I'll name her Maggie. If it's a boy, it's George," they all burst into laughter.

"Maggie, it's time for you to consider opening your next location," said George seriously.

"I know, I know, you're right. I shouldn't be scared of that," said Maggie hesitantly.

"It's okay to have a loving heart and a smart brain, Maggie," said Frankie. "Heart–mind connection makes you a superwoman," she said as she winked at George. Then she walked up to Maggie and handed her an envelope: "Here is a gift from George and me. An early Christmas present."

Maggie was about to speak before Frankie stopped her, "No, no, no until I finish," she said with motherly authority. "It's a weekend away in Wyoming, at the secluded," she paused to sound dramatic, "Intergalactic Ranch! It seems like a small, quiet place, and you can pick your own cabin. They even offer past life readings, energy work, massages, homemade organic breakfast, lunch, and dinner, so you don't have to drive anywhere. We got you the whole package."

"When George and I read about it, it sounded as crazy as your place here, and we thought this could be the perfect place for you to plan the next journey for Maggie's Beings and your life. Maggie, we all know you hardly take time for yourself. You will franchise Maggie. Just imagine how many people's lives will change for the better. Stop being afraid of your own power," Frankie was almost teary, so she added jokingly, "And just imagine how much more merchandise and art I will sell when you do that."

"I do not know what to say," tears of happiness escaped Maggie's eyes, "Thank you, thank you both so much. It all started with you, George. Thank you."

"No, Maggie," said George humbly. "It all started with you. When you found the courage to open your coffee shop, against all odds, you made it. You changed our lives, and we are happy to be here for you."

WYOMING
Mikael's Life

Maggie checked out a rental car at the airport and drove to her destination. She had to smile when she saw the "Intergalactic Ranch" sign, with the infinity symbol below, saying: Where the past ends, the future begins.

She continued slowly on the dirt road toward the main house. She parked, got out of the car, and was smitten with the beauty of nature.

A lovely woman in sportswear walked out of the house.

"Hi, I am Katy. You must be Maggie. Our new guest."

"How did you know?" laughed Maggie. She instantly liked Katy.

"Sixth sense," Katy said jokingly as she showed her to the dining room.

"Let me force some freshly baked scones on you and brew you a cup of coffee or tea. And then I'll show you around the ranch before I take you to your cabin."

"Make yourself comfortable," added Katy.

"You have a lovely place here. Have you always lived here?" asked Maggie.

"I wish, but no, "replied Katy. "My brother and I moved here two years ago from New York City when he bought this land. This main house was already here; we upgraded it a little, and since the land was already surveyed and approved for three cabins, we built them and turned a dream into a business. Mikael named them Sirius, Orion, and Pleiades."

Maggie smiled, "Those are unusual names for your cabins, even your ranch."

"True," nodded Katy, "But we love it."

"I do, too," Maggie quickly added.

"It's a long story about why he named it the way he did; maybe Mikael will share that with you. I just say, three years ago, he dreamt that he was flying to Orion, and here we are today."

"My life changed three years ago, too. Interesting," said Maggie softly.

"Speak of the devil. Here he is," said Katy cheerfully. As the door opened, a handsome man walked in.

"Mikael, what took you so long? You know I still have to cook dinner, and it's hard to do without groceries," she scolded him, "Do you want to have a cup of coffee with us?"

"Geez, Katy, you're gonna make us all addicts. But who am I to say no?"

He turned his gaze toward Maggie. Something flickered in his eyes as he extended his hand to hers. "I'm Mikael. Welcome to Intergalactic Ranch."

"Maggie," she managed to say with a bit of surprise as she extended her hand to his.

Sparks flew when their palms met. She knew those green eyes. How is this possible, she thought. They just stared at each other while their hands were connected.

Katy broke the silence with a strange look, "It seems this is not the first time you've met?"

"It's my first time in waking life. I've dreamt about you," said Mikael excitedly, shaking his head. "A few times. And judging from your surprised look, you must remember our meetings, too."

Maggie blushed and pulled her hand back, "I do. This is surreal."

Mikael did not want to scare her or make her uncomfortable, "People meet for a reason, don't you think? There must be a reason why you are here, Maggie. I know it seems awkward as we just met, but I feel like I've known you for such a long time."

"Coffee is ready, and blueberry scones with it," sang Katy happily, taking a sip of coffee. She made a sound of pure pleasure when she took her first sip. "This is my absolute favorite," she chirped.

Maggie sipped her coffee. "Is this Maggie's Beings coffee?" she asked, shocked.

"Yep, Mikael got me hooked on it. Now, we serve nothing else. After all, it's perfectly fitting to enjoy Maggie's Beings at the Intergalactic Ranch."

Maggie burst out laughing and could not stop. Stress, shock, tiredness, and happiness all exploded inside her. Katy and Mikael looked a little perplexed, and then Katy said, unsure, "I am sorry if we are being weird, but it just feels like we know you. I swear we can be very professional."

"Oh, no, you are fine," she said amid laughter. "I'm Maggie," she managed to say.

"We know, you told us," said Mikael.

"I mean, I'm the founder of Maggie's Beings. I thought I was the only weird one, and I was so worried about what people would think of that name, but seeing that my "beings" made it here before me, it was a sign to help me make my decision."

"Incredible," whispered Mikael.

"Wow, that is all I can say." Katy was surprised by this new development.

"So what brought you here, Maggie?" Mikael asked.

Katy was deep in her mind and thought out loud instead of letting Maggie answer, "Well, she is staying in Orion. She has some darkness to battle, let go of the past, and make decisions regarding the future."

"Do you read minds, Katy?" Maggie asked, relaxed. She did not feel insulted at all. She instantly liked both of them.

"No, that's Mikael's talent, I just read energy," she said thoughtfully.

"The Groceries are put away, and I can take care of cooking for tonight if you want me to," a husky voice yelled from the kitchen.

"Thank you, John," Katy yelled back.

"That's my husband," she winked at Maggie. I better go help him. Catch you two later. Mikael, can you show Maggie her cabin when she is ready, please?"

"Of course."

"So what kind of decision do you have to make?" he caught her off guard.

"Can't you just read my mind?" she teased.

"I prefer to ask than to snoop in your head. There is an ethical code for what I can do," said Mikael.

Maggie could not help but feel attracted to him. Talking to him was so easy; it was as if they hadn't seen each other for a while, but when they met, they just picked up where they had left off. She never felt like that with a man before.

"I was hoping to meet you, Maggie."

He must be married like his sister, she thought, quickly correcting herself. She better watch herself.

"So, what decision do you have to make?" he asked again, breaking the silence intentionally. He knew he would be wooing her, and it did not matter if it took a whole lifetime.

"I would like to franchise Maggie's Beings, but I need to be confident that this is the right direction for my people and me. It doesn't have to be huge, but I want it to be successful. People's jobs and future depend on me making the right decision."

"Maggie, did Katy tell you what I did before I bought this ranch?"

"No."

He started to laugh, "I am a financial expert. For years, my job was to help my clients find the best investment and plan for their financial success and retirement. I always wondered why I picked that job. Now I know. It is funny how life works."

"I think I can help you if you would like that. You are staying for the weekend, right?"

"Yes," she was surprised again.

"Oh, what the heck. This is like a family reunion, isn't it?" he added.

She just nodded.

"Except you and I are not brother and sister in this family, and I only hope you are single as I am."

She nodded her head again since she was speechless.

"If you like, I can show you around the place, and we can discuss the pros and cons of your possible franchise so you can make an informed decision," he cleared his throat. We have a whole weekend to hang out together if you like. You'll have to try the hot springs; they will blow your mind."

Then, in a serious voice, he added, "Maggie, I want to help you with your franchise. It's something I used to be very good at. You won't owe me anything. I want to do this because I feel that it's the right thing to do. Sounds good?" He extended his hand.

She hugged him instead of taking his hand, "Thank you," she whispered.

"We have more guests," yelled Katy, "Mikael, throw me the keys to Sirius."

"So, what kind of people stay in Sirius?" Maggie asked Mikael.

"Let's see, it looks like a young couple, probably just dating. On Sirius, you have to find unity between feminine and masculine energy. If they are not true to their feelings about each other or are playing a power game of who will control the other, they will last only one night. They will probably have a fight, maybe even break up," he shrugged.

Maggie smiled, "That's not good for business."

"If they listen to their intuition, it saves them from years of being unhappy in a relationship. It may not be good for business, but it should help them. On the other hand, if you last the whole weekend, your relationship should be bulletproof."

Maggie raised her eyebrows.

"Relationships are work. Honesty, acceptance, and communication with one another are important. You have to learn to be yourself instead of being someone who your boyfriend or girlfriend, or anyone for that matter, would want you to be."

"Wisdom and truth," she added.

"You got it."

Just then, another car pulled in, and a family in their late thirties with a tiny, skinny little girl walked out. Maggie thought she could be about three years old.

She looked at Mikael, whose face had just gone white.

"Are you okay?" she gently touched his arm. He looked like he had just seen a ghost.

As the family walked in, Mikael just stood there in silence. Katy was nowhere close by, so Maggie took it upon herself to greet them.

"Welcome to the Intergalactic Ranch. Did you have a pleasant drive here?"

"It was wonderful, thank you," smiled the woman.

Mikael just stared at the child, and she looked at him with the same intensity. Maggie was trying to figure out what to do.

She offered, "Would you like to have a cup of tea or coffee and scones before you head to your cabin?"

"Tea would be lovely, thank you," said the lady.

"This is Mikael, the owner of the ranch. He is a nice guy," she added, wondering if Mikael looked like a weirdo right now.

"Immie?" he finally managed to get one word out. She was the spitting image of his alien friend Immie. It had been a while since he saw her last.

"This is Ema," said the woman. "She is usually very shy around strangers, but for some reason, she is smitten with you."

"Does she remind you of someone?" Ema's mother said to Mikael.

At that moment, Ema saw a black cat walking in and turned her focus to her.

"I'm sorry, my name is Mikael. Welcome to the Intergalactic Ranch. Yes, she reminds me of someone I knew."

"My name is Mason, and this is my wife, Kelly. It's nice to meet you," said Mason.

"If you don't mind me asking, how did you find us?" Mikael asked.

Maggie served tea and scones while the family settled on the sofa. "You will think I am crazy," she said as she looked at her husband. He just smiled, "Just tell them."

"I was thinking of getting away for a few days, and I had a dream that we would go to the Intergalactic

Ranch. I thought it was just a dream, but I googled the name, and you showed up on the radar."

"I am glad you are here," smiled Mikael.

At that moment, Ema had a tiny seizure, and Kelly held her in her lap.

"Is she okay?" Maggie asked worryingly." Can we do something?"

"Thank you. She will be fine in a little bit," said Kelly as she took a deep breath and, relying on intuition, continued. "Ema has Dravet syndrome."

Judging by their looks, Kelly knew they had no idea what Dravet syndrome was. She continued, "She has a rare form of epilepsy that causes prolonged seizures. Many children with this condition regress after each seizure they have. So far, we are fortunate that Ema doesn't have the same symptoms as the other children. We have done our best to give her the best outcome. She only has very small seizures every few weeks; they do stress us out, but we are so grateful to have such a wonderful daughter; we feel fortunate to have her."

"Is there a cure?" asked Mikael.

"No. But there are medicines that keep her seizures under control," said Kelly while holding her husband's hand. She felt so comfortable here. She did not mind sharing all of this with perfect strangers.

"How old is she?" Mikael asked.

"She is going to be five this weekend, and for some reason, we wanted to celebrate her birthday here—just us. She is so precious, and I feel so hopeless that I can't save my little princess from this," Mason's voice shook a little.

Just then, Mikael saw what he needed to see. It was so clear. When Ema had a seizure, Immie was like an auric twin next to her body. Immie looked at him, and telepathically, he heard, "Help me, please." At that moment, Mikael knew the whole story of Immie.

Immie was incarnated on Earth as Ema, but she needed to integrate her higher ET energy to fit Ema's little body. She will be five this weekend, which is the number of transformations. When she tried to do it on her own, Ema's electric system (her nervous system) glitched. Ema is Immie. Ema may not fully remember Immie, but she will heal, help others heal, and integrate into life on Earth.

This land, this Intergalactic land, was prepared for star-seeds like her to heal. Immie's soul had guided Mr. Miller's father, a star-seed with a broken heart, to purchase this land so that he may heal from the land's healing energy and, at the same time, preserve the land for other starseed who may need its healing. Once healed, with a pure heart and clear mind, Mr. Miller's father became a successful businessman who never forgot the gift he had received and always paid it forward. Then, three years ago, Immie appeared to Mikael in a dream and began preparing him to become the guardian of the land so that he may use it to serve others. Mikael realized that for many who visit this land, the past ends here, and the future begins.

"I believe I know why you were guided here," said Mikael, "Someone that I knew guided your dreams to find us. Everything has a reason and explanation. Do you believe that?" he asked them.

"Actually, I do believe in that. Everything happens for a reason," answered Kelly.

"I hope that while you are here, you plan on soaking in our hot springs. They are actually closest to your cabin." He reached into his pocket and took out the green stone that Immie showed him three years ago. The stone that Katy bought for him.

"If you are open to a little magic experiment, borrow this stone. But please know there are no guarantees that this will work."

"Is this Moldavite?" Mason asked.

"Yes, it is. Let Ema hold it today, play with it for a while, and then both of you hold it and feel its energy," he looked at Mason and Kelly, "Hold the stone in your hand and tell it the condition that Ema has, and what kind of help she needs. Then, bury it overnight by the tree's roots closest to your cabin so the Earth can program it with the healing energy it needs. Tomorrow, when you go to the hot springs, take the stone with you and have it in the water with you. The water will be infused with its healing energy. When you are done, let the stone sit in the sun by your cabin or on the windowsill. Then, on Saturday night, do the same thing, bury the stone, and enjoy it on Sunday. And please, before you leave, bring the stone back to me. It has sentimental value to me."

He handed the stone to Kelly.

"Thank you so much. I am speechless. We appreciate this so much. I do not know why, but I feel like we have known you for such a long time. I feel that Ema will be fine."

"And here," he grabbed something from the counter, "My sister says this helps keep the stone from being lost in the water." He handed her a netted pouch necklace they were selling at the ranch alongside Katy's crystal collection.

"Thank you."

"The magic of healing comes when you least expect it. Let your past end here, and when you walk out of the hot springs, may your future begin. Enjoy your weekend. I will ask Katy to make Ema's birthday cake. This is a new beginning for all of us," he looked at the little girl.

"Happy Birthday, Ema!"

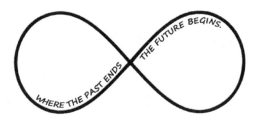

ABOUT THE AUTHOR

Eva Marquez is a spiritual consultant, soul healer, guide, teacher, TM Sidha, and writer with a Pleiadian starseed lineage. She has authored six books and appeared on Gaia TV's "Beyond Belief." She works alongside her guides, the Lights of the Universe, a group of light beings from different star nations, including the Pleiades. In her spiritual practice, she draws on Pleiadian energy, the Language of Light, and other ancient soul memories.

Eva and her team help starseeds remember their past lives on Earth and beyond, activate their dormant cosmic DNA, and reconnect with their soul family. She strives to aid starseeds in adapting to their physical bodies, empowering them to fulfill their life missions in supporting humanity's evolution into a multidimensional species while safeguarding the planet for future generations.

Eva brings the memories of infinite love – the essence of God's Source – the most profound energy that is your original essence. She walks beside you on your life journey, assisting you in letting go of your fears of darkness and limitations and seeing the light at the end of the tunnel. Ultimately, she guides you to the point where infinite love is no longer a memory but your guide. Infinite love will become your friend on the journey toward the light of your origin. Love and light give birth to the wisdom that is a compass for the soul-mind consciousness on the healing journey of returning home to its original source. It is Eva's greatest wish that you find your way home.

Learn more about Eva and her services and classes:
www.EvaMarquez.org

Visit Eva's YouTube channel: Eva Marquez

OTHER BOOKS BY EVA MARQUEZ

One Last Thing

If you liked this book, I would be grateful if you could leave a brief review on Amazon. Your support means a lot to me, and I read every review. Thank you for being so supportive!

Love and Light,
Eva Marquez

Made in the USA
Las Vegas, NV
04 September 2024

94804856R00125